the new *Dream* *interpreter*

the new Dream interpreter

mehr-ali kalami

from the original writings of
Hossein Kalami

quantum

LONDON • NEW YORK • TORONTO • SYDNEY

quantum

an imprint of W. Foulsham & Co. Ltd
The Publishing House, Bennetts Close, Cippenham, Slough,
Berkshire SL1 5AP, England

ISBN 0-572-02617-X

Printed in Great Britain by St. Edmundsbury Press, Bury St. Edmund, Suffolk

Acknowledgements

Hossein Kalami met many researchers while preparing this book and acknowledges the support and learning of the following:

Hamid Ibn Qader (1850–1946)

Karim Ibn Shafagh (1845–1944)

Jaafar Ibn Ibrahim (d. 1945)

Jassem Ibn Sarraf (d. 1946)

Mohammad Ibn Rasool (d. 1943)

Hakim Mohammad Jaafar Kuhestani (1848–1938)

Guru Baldev Singh Chaddah (d. 1930)

Harish Chand Babu

Maulana Faiz Ahmad (1850–1947)

Hakim Mehmet Rahmanoglou (d. 1947)

Hakim Burhan Beig (d. 1946)

Introduction

People have always been fascinated by the workings of the subconscious mind and, therefore, by the significance and interpretation of dreams. This work is designed to give you a new insight into the prophetic meanings of your dreams as they may be applied to your waking life.

A clear explanation of the process of dreaming can be found in the work of Hamid Ibn Qader, a respected master of dream interpretation.

'Virtually everyone is inwardly aware that there are deep connections between a human being's activities in his subconscious state and whatever he sees in this subconscious world. We can also say that certain impersonal forces over which we do not appear to have any sort of control are the ones that go to create a dream. These forces set to work once our conscious state is deactivated (we sleep) to a certain extent, but not lapsing into a total or an absolute state of deactivation or deep sleep where the state of mind enters a temporary period of total blankness. The absolute state of deactivation renders the mental faculty fully blank during the subconscious state and hence prevents the formation of an image, whereas a semi-deactivated state is able to create the conditions that go to form a dream.'

Another acknowledged expert, Hakim Burhan Beig, explains his interpretation of the importance of dreams to our lives:

'Time and again over the centuries, it has been proved that a clearly recalled dream essentially signals messages either encouraging or otherwise and even signs of guidance on which we can accordingly alter our activities to utilise fully the possibilities seemingly awaiting us.

'In case we forget or misinterpret, it is definitely the dreamer and no other person who finally infers as to whether the dream bears with it, if at all, any message or sign worthy of prophetic significance.'

This collection of modern dream interpretation was compiled by Hossein Kalami (1857–1950). He was born in a small village called Eishabad, some 16 kilometres (10 miles) south of the desert city of

Yazd in central Iran. Hossein's father, Hassan, who died in 1918, was an illiterate farmer who used to interpret dreams for the other villagers whenever the opportunity arose.

Hossein, after gaining some rudimentary knowledge, made in-depth studies of the Koran and attended theology classes in Kerman, in south-central Iran, and at the Chahar Bagh Theology Centre in Isfahan. While he was studying, he began to be fascinated by the subject of interpreting dreams. By the time he returned to his home town, his interest in the subject had deepened and he began to make it the subject of serious studies. He wrote:

> 'By the grace of the Almighty, in the year 1280 of the Persian calendar which equals to 1901 of the Christian calendar, I was some 40 years old and I decided to make extensive studies in analysing dreams. Consequently, I had the opportunity to travel to several countries in the region. I travelled to several cities in India, some of which are now in Pakistan, and also to Iraq, Syria and Turkey. There I met several honoured masters, who are later named, to acquire their views and opinions concerning the hidden mysteries and the various significances of dreams.

> 'I have prepared these writings from more than four decades of exhaustive consultations, research and exchange of views with the masters. The interpretations may not appear identical to those expounded by other writers and scholars.'

That fact that different sources give different interpretations of dreams is something that interests those who believe in dream interpretation but that also allows the sceptics to criticise. However, the subject of interpretation is not a perfect science. The interpretations in this book are based on experiences accumulated through consultations, arguments and discussions of traditional beliefs, coupled with an understanding of modern social conditions. They are an accurate and authoritative reflection of the author's research, but readers must bring their own logic, reason, arguments and understanding to the application of the text to their own lives. It is certainly clear that each of us is an individual and we have our own unique memories, thoughts and feelings. In interpreting a dream, our conscious experience is bound to have an effect both on our subconscious itself, and also in the interpretation of what we have experienced.

A frequently asked question is whether we have any control over our dreams. From research, it seems that it may certainly be possible to influence them to some degree. However, before attempting such a thing, a person must be able, through strenuous concentration and meditation, to clear their mind completely of negative emotions such as revenge or anger and achieve a totally relaxed mental state before going to sleep. In many such cases, at least a faint message directly or indirectly manifests itself in dreams.

Finally, there are dreams that are caused by an external, physical influence, such as pain or overeating. These dreams are said to be 'organic' and have no prophetic significance.

The profoundness of the impression that dreams can have upon an individual – whether it is an extremely delightful and satisfying event or one filled with indications of anguish or misery – essentially leaves that dream permanently etched on the mind. This collection is designed to offer some insight into the significance of those dream experiences.

Abandonment Any form of abandonment symbolises a break in friendship and intellectual problems.

You abandon someone Abandoning a child suggests a stormy period arising out of carelessness, while abandoning your partner means you have an unrealistic approach to life. Abandoning a friend or animal emphasises the existence of emotional problems in your life.

Someone abandons you If you are abandoned by your parents or a partner, it indicates deep misunderstandings within the family.

Abbeys *see* **Monasteries**

Abbots To dream of an abbot indicates good health and prosperity.

An abbot giving you something If the abbot gives you anything, whether or not it is worthless, it suggests you will regain lost health and emotional strength.

Giving something to an abbot This indicates good health and prosperity for you.

An abbot lecturing you Within the next few days you will benefit from someone's advice and this will change your way of life for the better.

Speaking to an abbot You are likely to gain the confidence of those around you. If you are in business, you will gain further prosperity.

Abdomens A normal abdomen symbolises health and also that you are a modest and careful person.

Blood dripping from your abdomen If the amount of blood is small, this indicates that your problems will increase unless you move quickly to prevent this happening. If the amount of blood is unrealistically great, this is an organic, not a prophetic, dream (see page 9).

Healed scars on the abdomen You will be able to prevent any general setback if you are cautious in your way of life.

Wounds in the abdomen You are likely to undergo a short period of illness unless you seek professional guidance.

Abysses An abyss or bottomless pit of any kind symbolises dangers, possibly a little way in the future. It can also indicate unbearable pain and suffering resulting mainly from your own faults and carelessness.

Falling into an abyss As the saying goes: 'Crime does not pay'. You have probably done something illegal, immoral or just plain hurtful and inconsiderate, and you are reaping the rewards of your bad behaviour.

Standing over or looking down an abyss This is a warning of dangers around you. You should replan your objectives in life or face disproportionately negative consequences. You need to take a wiser, more thoughtful approach to your lifestyle in order to improve your attitude to your situation and those around you.

Accidents An accident in a dream symbolises possible or impending danger.

A vehicle accident You may encounter an unexpected mishap in your home life.

An accident involving an animal Do not take any business risks unless you are sure of good results.

An accident involving you Following such a dream, you should be very careful in what you plan and where you go. If you are in a car or train when the accident occurs, it is an indication that you should postpone any business travel.

Injuring a person or an animal in an accident You could be heading for a financial loss.

Accountants To dream of an accountant symbolises justice, although the interpretations vary depending on the circumstances. If you recognise the accountant, this is generally a good sign for your business or work-related affairs.

Being an accountant This is a good dream, suggesting your honest behaviour will finally lead you to better days as a result of other people's increased confidence in your abilities.

Being introduced to an accountant Good fortune will come your way and you will achieve your objectives sooner than you had anticipated.

Being summoned by an accountant If you are called by an accountant and you feel guilty, you are hiding something which could cause you problems.

Calling an accountant If you dream of making an appointment for business reasons, this means that you will make your living through your own efforts, perhaps setting up a small business that will turn out to be modestly successful.

Arguing with an accountant Having dreamt this, you should review both your business and your personal circumstances.

Acne Acne, spots or pimples on the face symbolise hardship and problems arising out of jealousy.

Acne on your face If you do not actually have acne, it means that people you have trusted as friends will betray you. Take steps to ensure that their actions do not place you on the wrong side of the law. If you do have acne and you also dream of having it, it suggests that you are an honest person and have nothing to hide.

Other people with acne Whether or not the people you dream of have acne in real life, this dream suggests that they are unreasonably jealous of you. Try to make sure they have no reason to feel that way.

Acquittal *see* **Innocence**

Admiration Admiration for an object or an individual in one's dream symbolises contentment and inner calm.

Admiring an object Whether or not the object has any artistic value, it suggests either that you are undergoing a period of calm and tranquillity, or that in the near future you will achieve some of your modest aims.

Admiring someone of the same sex You have the qualities you need to develop your personality.

Admiring someone of the opposite sex Such a dream strongly suggests that you are very satisfied with your family, especially your partner and your children.

Being admired by other people Your presence has proved beneficial to society in some way. It also means that you have a lucky time ahead of you.

Aeroplanes Aeroplanes or other flying objects can symbolise both favourable and unfavourable developments, depending on the circumstances in which they appear in your dream. In general, this is a good dream, unless you have been up to no good.

A low-flying aeroplane You are contented with life in general.

A high-flying aeroplane You may expect promotion or financial gain at work or a positive and pleasant response to something you have been expecting. If you are out of work, it suggests an employment opportunity in the near future. If you have been engaging in illegal activities, however, prepare for a period of activity followed by a sudden downfall, perhaps ending in legal action against you.

An aeroplane taxiing on a runway This dream is a sign of encouragement to pursue your goals since they appear to be taking you in the right direction.

An aeroplane taking off You have every right to believe in your cause, which will ultimately lead you to achieve your ambitions.

A crashed aeroplane If you are at some distance from the crash, this dream denotes you need to do some careful planning or risk being involved in losses of some kind, possibly financial. If, however, you are very near to the wreckage, it signifies your dissatisfaction with your present situation due to problems created by unscrupulous people around you.

Being in an aeroplane about to take off You may soon undertake a short and fruitful journey.

Flying in an aeroplane This indicates that all your hard work will pay off.

Being in a falling aeroplane This suggests losses due to your indecision and nerves. If the craft appears to regain its height, it indicates a setback in business or domestic affairs that is only temporary.

Being in a taxiing aeroplane You can have confidence in your friends.

See also **Pilots**

Aircraft *see* **Aeroplanes**

Alligators *see* **Crocodiles**

Alms *see* **Charity**

Altars Altars in a dream can signify happiness or unhappiness, depending on the circumstances.

Facing an altar and praying If you are feeling happy, this signifies that happiness and good fortune will be yours in the near future. If you are unhappy in the dream, this can herald a difficult period in your life, perhaps even the loss of a loved one.

Anchors This dream can have good or bad connotations, depending on the circumstances.

An anchor on land Your activities are heading for a standstill and you are likely to encounter difficulties ahead. You may be refusing to accept the realities of life. However, if a rope or chain is attached to the anchor, this indicates that by your own perseverance you will overcome the difficulties and get back on the right course.

An anchor in water If the anchor is not attached to anything and is lying at the bottom of the sea or lake, it signifies that you may receive bad news, perhaps of illness or even death in the family.

An anchor in water attached to a boat If you can see the anchor clearly, it indicates that you are personally responsible for the problems that have recently slowed your progress. Nevertheless, you will overcome those problems through your own efforts.

A ship lowering its anchor If the water is clear and you can see the anchor being lowered, there are fairly good chances that you will prosper in life. If the water is murky, however, this means that circumstances are against you for the moment.

An anchor being pulled up from the seabed This dream indicates that tremendous opportunities are open to you and if you grasp them and use them constructively you will be able to develop your talents.

Angels The presence of an angel in a dream symbolises happiness and success in realising the major goals in your life. If you are married, you will enjoy an excellent married life. If you are unmarried, you will find a loving and devoted partner.

An angel close to you or talking to you There are better things to come. If you have been ill, you will recover; if you have suffered financial difficulties, your circumstances will improve.

An angel scolding you You should be more cautious in your emotional relationships with friends and those around you.

Anger This is generally an unfavourable dream signifying financial loss, stress or betrayal.

You are angry If you are angry at work in your dream, you may experience problems at work or even unemployment difficulties. If you show anger towards your friends or partner, then arguments with them are likely.

Others are angry with you This often indicates that you are at fault in some way and may find difficulties at work or at home.

Ants Ants are a symbol of honesty and perseverance. If you see a column of ants in your dream, you are likely to find happiness in your life. A single ant is a symbol of encouragement.

A dead ant Rivals or enemies are out to harm you.

A flying ant You have a fruitful journey ahead, although you will not necessarily gain financially.

An ant carrying a grain or leaf You have a strong sense of spirituality.

Holding an ant You are an honest person.

Killing an ant You have a tendency to be vengeful.

Anxiety Anxiety in a dream does not necessarily foretell unhappiness in real life.

Anxiety in yourself If you feel anxious in your dream, it indicates that you are worrying about a sudden change in your life, which will turn out to be for the better. It also indicates that you are unwilling to consider any changes to your plans, whatever the outcome may be. Don't concern yourself too much about what is happening in your life.

Anxiety in others You are likely to attain a respectable and responsible position in life and you will be able to help and guide others in positive directions.

Apples Apples generally symbolise health, wealth and happiness, although rotten apples denote a short period of ill-feeling with your immediate family.

A basket of apples This denotes a successful business career.

Buying apples Visitors will greatly enhance your potential for success.

Eating apples A long and healthy life is in store for you.

Picking apples You will have a happy married life.

Being given apples You will either receive an expensive gift or be given ample support to advance yourself at work or even to start a new business.

Apricots If you are unmarried, you will soon find a marriage partner or will decide to marry your present partner.
Buying apricots You want to end a period of isolation.
Eating apricots You are likely to marry within a year.
Picking apricots You have a positive attitude to life that will serve you well.

Arguments The interpretation of this dream varies depending on the situation and the person with whom you are arguing.
Arguing with a person of the same gender You may have a temporary setback in your professional activities.
Arguing with a person of the opposite gender There is a degree of misunderstanding in your personal relationships, perhaps leading to a temporary break with your partner.
Arguing with your parents This is a warning to be less aggressive in your behaviour or the results of your actions will not be favourable to you.
Arguing defiantly You have the ability to defend yourself and hence you will be able to minimise the negative effects.
See also **Anger, Insults**

Armaments *see* **Weapons**

Armies This is another dream with different interpretations depending on the circumstances.
An army on a ceremonial parade Such a dream heralds a possible celebration by you or someone in your family. If the soldiers are armed, the celebration will have special significance. It could also mean the end of a bitter period for you personally.
An army in retreat This does not necessarily mean defeat for you, but it does indicate a change in your life. Surprisingly, this is usually for the better and will be brought about through your own efforts. The logic is that the army that has retreated in defeat will reorganise itself and prepare with renewed zeal for another attempt at victory. If you do experience failure, it will be short-lived and temporary.
A tired but undefeated army This signifies an imminent loss of property or an unexpected loss in your financial affairs. If the solders are wounded and bandaged or on stretchers, it can indicate severe difficulties in your family, perhaps related to serious illness.

An army group welcoming you Take this dream as an inspiration to overcome any problems you are experiencing. Your problems are not as great as you have imagined and you can solve them.

An army group relaxing You need to rest to overcome either mental or physical exhaustion.

A heavily armed group awaiting battle orders Be on your guard against jealous individuals around you.

Two armies in combat Such a dream often indicates a period of anxiety. It also underscores your stubborn nature and your refusal to face the bitter facts of life. If there is a sudden ceasefire in the dream, friends or relatives will intervene to help you out of a difficult situation.

See also **Fighting, Soldiers, Wars**

Arrest This is a dream of contrary indication, in that arrest of any kind in a dream does not necessarily symbolise the dreamer's impending detention in real life but can be interpreted as a sign of being held safe and away from harm.

You are arrested but not taken into custody You are likely to extricate yourself single-handedly from your domestic entanglements. If you are experiencing a financial setback, your own honest efforts will help you.

You are arrested and remanded in custody Not only will you triumph over your difficulties very soon but you will also be safe from any severe or extreme problems or developments.

See also **Police Officers, Prison**

Arrows An arrow symbolises a tense period marked with unhappiness.

Shooting an arrow Such a dream underlines your unhappy, isolated or despairing situation. You feel you have lost control of your circumstances, which possibly even appear completely hopeless. You need to find ways to control your emotions, through meditation or other means. Then you will be in a position to think and plan carefully to change your unfortunate circumstances.

Being shot by an arrow Erratic behaviour will cause you sorrow or loss. Take the advice of those older or wiser than yourself and you will be in a better position to get out of difficulty.

Ash Ash in dreams symbolises destruction and an end to a cycle of life.

Ash all around you Your life's goal will ultimately be achieved, even if you have to wait for success.

Ash on your body Such a dream signifies the end of a particular cycle of your life. You may be about to change your profession, get a new job or change your situation in some other way, although it does not necessarily mean that you will gain financially by the changes. The gain will be spiritual or emotional.

See also **Fire**

Assassins Dreams about assassins are associated with bad news.

An assassin comes close to you If an assassin comes near you and threatens you but does not harm you, it is a sign of impending problems that may strongly affect your daily life. It may also indicate a forthcoming accident or illness, or financial loss if you are about to embark on a business deal. Try to avoid long-distance travel or finalising business deals for at least a week.

An assassin stabs you and escapes Quarrels are predicted by such a dream, perhaps even violent ones in which you are wounded. The less blood you see in the dream, the more dangerous the potential outcome, although establishing a calm frame of mind through relaxation and meditation should enable you to overcome the impending difficulties.

See also **Killing**

B

Babies Babies in dreams denote success and prosperity in all your affairs, whether they be business or personal.

A new-born baby This is an auspicious sign symbolising good health, success and happiness.

A crying baby This indicates a new life and new beginnings.

A woman holding a baby If you are unmarried, this dream indicates a marriage in the near future. If you are already married or in a long-term relationship, it suggests that you have an excellent relationship with your partner.

A man holding a baby Petty misunderstandings will create uneasiness within the family. If you are married, practise restraint and be prepared to compromise.

A married couple with their baby This indicates happiness and successful relationships with your partner. If you are ill, you are likely to recover quickly.

See also **Birth**

Bags Bags symbolise favourable developments, usually financial.

A bag held in your hand Whether the bag is empty or full, it denotes a sudden change for the better, usually involving financial gain. If you are holding a bag containing money or something of value, you can expect a satisfying end to your projects or aspirations. If you are employed or in business, it means money from a source you least expect.

A bag on the ground Especially if the bag is closed, this is an encouraging sign to go ahead with any small business projects.

A bag on a table, bed or chair You will acquire sudden riches through an inheritance.

See also **Luggage**

Bakers A baker in a dream symbolises the arrival of good news and the satisfactory results of hard work.

Being a baker You will be offered a new employment opportunity, which will be to your advantage.

Seeing a baker in the street This indicates that your work will soon come to fruition.

Seeing a baker at work This is an even stronger indication that you will be rewarded for your efforts. If you see the baker

working with the dough, it means very good news is on the way, perhaps something that will change the course of your life.
Giving something to a baker You will receive surprise news, often pleasant.
Receiving something from a baker Good luck is just around the corner.
Having an argument with a baker A sudden mishap will occur due to your negligence.

Balconies These dreams have different interpretations depending on the circumstances.
Standing on a balcony If you are alone, this indicates a considerable and well-deserved promotion. If you are with friends or family, you will further gain the confidence of friends, family and colleagues. If you are with your business partner, it means an unexpected gain in your business dealings.
Falling from a balcony This suggests that you must be careful not to experience difficulties caused by your own extravagance, or perhaps because you have not operated entirely within the law. This is a dream likely to be experienced by someone who has been corrupt or unscrupulous, particularly in business affairs.

Baldness Baldness in a dream is generally unfavourable as it symbolises loss.
Seeing bald men This dream is a warning to be alert and careful in your dealings.
Seeing bald women This suggests that you are gradually slipping into the habit of doubtful, immoral or even illegal behaviour.
Being bald (men) If you are not bald but you have this dream, it foretells losses and worries arising out of your own dubious activities. If you are really bald, it is a sign that you should refrain from any wrong-doing as it will cost you dearly.
Being bald (women) You may be tempted to undertake some activity which will make you rich, even though you know it may be unscrupulous, immoral or even illegal.

Bananas Seeing bananas in a dream symbolises a sense of isolation.
Buying bananas You may be limiting your own horizons by your attitude to life. You are capable of achieving more if you want.

Eating bananas You are modest and unassuming.
Offering bananas This indicates your basic honesty.
Picking bananas You have a reticent and careful nature.

Bandits *see* **Criminals**

Banquets Banquets in dreams symbolise future prosperity and
wealth.
Attending a banquet You will very soon witness the fruits of
your hard work. If you are alone in the dream, you will solve
your immediate problems alone. If you are accompanied by
someone, it indicates a joint business venture with a trustworthy
person.
Giving a banquet This is considered a rare dream experienced by
especially philanthropic people. If you are young, you may
inherit a large fortune. If you are engaged in business, it suggests
further prosperity, coupled with good health.
See also **Eating**

Barbers *see* **Hairdressers**

Baskets A basket in a dream is usually associated with financial
difficulties.
An empty basket If the basket is quite large and has holes in it,
it is a message advocating caution and reticence in your business
or financial activities. If the empty basket is well made, however,
it indicates that you will achieve your goals, albeit with a
struggle.
Items in a basket If there is at least one object, no matter what
its value, in the basket, it means that a loss you are likely to
experience can be minimised or averted if you take sensible
action. If the basket is full, it symbolises a period of happiness
and good luck.
A covered basket A covered basket, which turns out to be
empty when you remove the cover, indicates that you will be
deceived by people whom you have considered to be your friends.
The smaller the basket, the smaller the effect of the resulting
problems.

Bathing Taking a bath in a dream symbolises the cleansing of
worries, whether financial or domestic.

Bathing in flowing water If the water is clean, it strongly suggests the immediate elimination of your major problems. If the water is murky or muddy, it means that any stress you are experiencing at the moment due to personal worries will lessen.

Taking a hot bath This dream generally indicates a satisfying result to your domestic problems. If another person appears to give you a bath, it indicates that encouragement from friends will help you improve your situation in life. If you are taking a bath with your clothes on, it is symptomatic of reckless behaviour in you.

Seeing others bathing Whether they are in a pond, river or public bath, seeing a group of men or women bathing indicates a change in your life. It may not be for the best, but it will make things better for you.

Bats Bats in dreams symbolise conspiracies and general setbacks. They can also indicate ill-health and arguments.

A flying bat Those around you may be working against you, or you may experience a short illness.

A roosting bat A short period of unhappiness is likely.

A bat on the ground A modest financial loss is likely.

A dead bat This is a sign of a general setback in your life.

Being attacked by a bat You are likely to quarrel with friends.

Killing a bat You are determined to isolate yourself from undesirable individuals around you.

Beans Depending on the quality of the food, the significance of this dream can be either good or bad.

Beans growing or ready to be cooked These symbolise success in business, a period of calm and general satisfaction in life.

Eating beans If the beans are uncooked, good health should follow this dream, or improved health for anyone who is ill. If they are cooked, it indicates that you will experience hard work just getting through the daily grind of hard work and may suffer some financial hardships.

Serving beans Serving beans to others means that you will quarrel with your friends or neighbours over petty matters.

Dried beans Seeing these in a dream suggests possible illness, which could worsen if you do not seek advice. Buying dried beans indicates acute financial problems.

Beards Different interpretations apply to dream of beards, depending on the circumstances.

Your own beard If you actually have a beard and dream of having one, your life will continue along much the same lines as it is at the moment. If you do not have a beard in real life, you must be careful that you do not cause yourself to be charged with fraud or be accused of some other criminal activity.

A man with a beard If the beard is short, it denotes a short period of success for you, followed by difficulties. If the beard is long and flowing, your success will enjoy more stability. If you recognise the man and he does not have a beard in real life, it suggests deceit and fraud will engulf you if you do not alter your lifestyle.

A woman with a beard This is an indication that your life is not as moral as it should be and you are tending towards criminal or immoral activity.

Bears A bear in a dream is often associated with animosity, ungratefulness and revenge.

A docile or friendly bear This is a warning to beware of hypocrites.

Being attacked by a bear Your enemies are conspiring against you.

Being frightened by a bear Expect problems created by untrustworthy acquaintances.

Frightening a bear You will be successful in foiling their plots.

Wounding a bear You are demonstrating a wish to change your life for the better.

Beds A bed in a dream symbolises idleness, sickness and financial setbacks, or it may suggest a short period marked with unhappiness.

Buying a bed This foretells the imminent arrival of good news.

Resting on a bed Any new project you are contemplating can be undertaken without difficulty. If you are covered with a blanket, however, it indicates illness, although not necessarily acute.

Sitting on a bed A fairly long period of financial difficulties or even unemployment is indicated.

Being asked to lie or sit on a bed This indicates you will soon enjoy a well-earned rest after a successful business deal. It may also signal a change for the better in your life. If you are unmarried or not in a relationship, the prospects for a new relationship appear to be favourable.

Bees Like ants, bees in a dream symbolise perseverance and truth.
A single bee This is an indication of prosperity.
Bees near their hive Gains through continued perseverance are indicated.
Bees on a flower You are wholly faithful to your partner.
A dead bee or killing a bee You are impatient.
See also **Honey**

Beggars Depending on the circumstances, these dreams can have favourable or unfavourable indications.
Being a beggar If you see yourself in rags and misery, it means, surprisingly, that you are encouraged to go ahead with whatever plans you have. Your plans are well structured and will bring you success, whether in business, travel or domestic circumstances.
Seeing a beggar This is a warning of impending bad news unless you move fast enough to control your emotions. If the beggar approaches you to speak with you, it means unhappy days are ahead.
Giving something to a beggar You are about to receive financial help from the quarter you least expect and you will experience a sudden rise in your prosperity. If you refuse to give anything, you will continue to lead the same life as at present.
A beggar giving you something This is an unfavourable dream. You will suffer a spectacular downfall due to your own arrogance. Look after your health and be considerate in your dealings with friends, family and colleagues. Postpone any new business ventures for the time being.

Bells In dreams, bells symbolise good news and indicate that better times are just round the corner, underlining your own perseverance in working towards a better standard of living. However, take care when embarking on new plans.
Hearing a bell ringing Your projects have been successful even though you may be unaware of it. You are likely to be rewarded more than you expect. A church bell often signifies sad news.
Ringing a bell This indicates that you are satisfied with life. It also means a happy married life. For those who are unmarried, it foretells a sudden meeting with your future partner in life.

Bicycles A bicycle symbolises our level of awareness of our own feelings. If you see a bicycle in a dream, it can denote a fickle nature, or simply that you are unsure of what you should be doing.
Riding a bicycle Such a dream means you are well aware of your actions. It does not definitely denote success in your endeavours, but it does not indicate any losses to come.
Being given a bicycle You can count on your friends for help. Also, decisive actions are necessary if you are to arrive at a satisfactory result. You cannot wait for things to happen, you must make them happen.

Birth As might be expected, a birth in a dream symbolises the beginning of a new and fruitful cycle in the dreamer's life.
Hearing of a birth If the birth is within your family, it indicates a resolution to any outstanding financial problems. Otherwise, it symbolises a general improvement in your affairs.
Witnessing a birth This means that a sudden transformation for the better awaits you. If you are married, it indicates that your partner and children will enjoy a happy and prosperous future. If you are employed, you can expect promotion. Whether or not you are employed, you can look forward to an employment opportunity.
See also **Babies, Pregnancy**

Black *see* **Colours**

Blackbirds Seeing a blackbird perched near your home is a warning of difficulties to come, from unemployment, financial problems or personal difficulties.

Blankets A blanket symbolises a cautious approach to life and the desire to prevent any difficulties.
Sitting on a blanket Sitting on a blanket means you are not fully utilising your talents or abilities in order to get the best out of life. You may be indifferent to any opportunities which come your way.
Being given a blanket You are respected by your friends and family and they want to help you.
Giving a blanket to someone You will achieve a comfortable status in life and will therefore be able to help others.

Blindness Blindness in a dream symbolises recklessness. If you continue with this sort of behaviour, it can lead to disappointments or worse.

Seeing a blind person This is a signal that you should take stock of your way of life and your behaviour. You are responsible for your own actions and cannot pretend that they have no effect on others. It may also indicate an impending financial problem.

Being blind This is a warning to take great care in your daily affairs and also to select your friends well and not be gullible. Not everyone has your best interests at heart.

Someone leading a blind person Take the good advice of friends or colleagues as they will be able to help you out of the difficulties into which you have got yourself.

See also **Eyes**

Blue *see* **Colours**

Board games Playing games such as chess, backgammon, Chinese checkers or draughts means that you will find opportunities shortly that will help you get what you want. If there are two people playing, expect things to happen soon.

See also **Chess**

Boats A rowing boat in a dream signifies hope and success. Seeing a rowing boat on calm water means that there are good, clear opportunities to achieve your goals. If the water is choppy, it means that it will be hard, but you will succeed in the end.

Rowing in a boat If you are alone, your own efforts will lead you to success. If you are with friends or family members, it means they will play a major role in your success. Their presence also means they have confidence in you.

See also **Canoes, Keels, Oars, Sailing, Ships, Sinking**

Bones Bones in a dream are often said to be associated with a nervous disposition, loss and even illness.

Animal bones Animal bones in a dream signify financial loss and domestic problems. Running away from the bones out of fright or disgust has no additional significance.

Human bones You will lose a very good friend as a result of your unbearable attitude. If the bones are scattered around, it underlines the fact that you feel, quite unreasonably, that everyone is against you and you are likely to accuse them wrongfully. A pile of human bones can indicate sickness.

Finding unidentified bones This dream reflects your violent temper and difficulties, misunderstandings or even quarrels in the family. For those who are married, a bitter disagreement is on the cards.

Being given a bone or bones Large financial losses are likely to follow this dream, but you have no one to blame but yourself. You will also lose your friends one by one because of your erratic behaviour.

See also **Skeletons, Skulls**

Books A book symbolises success and general good luck.

Seeing a book or books You have the potential within you to do well in life.

Buying a book This dream should encourage you to go ahead with your plans and promises the success of your modest wishes.

Being given a book Whether the book is new or old, this is a reminder that you have the confidence of friends and will receive every possible help and support from them.

Reading a book You will probably arrive at your goals alone and are likely to be successful if you are involved in any legal disputes. If you are reading a hand-written book or a newly printed book with an attractive cover, it is a sign of financial gains. However, if the book is shabby and falling apart, it can mean that you will experience emotional worries.

See also **Libraries**

Borders see **Frontiers**

Bottles The significance of a bottle in a dream depends on whether it is full or empty, large or small, its contents and colour and whether or not it is broken. It can therefore symbolise either prosperity or setbacks.

A large, empty bottle This signifies that you have an easy-going attitude to life which, if you are not careful, could become too laid-back for your own good.

A small bottle This dream reflects your fickle nature. Although there are times when you will be more serious and realistic, you generally suffer from a lack of determination.

*A **bottle full of drink*** A full bottle is a good sign of prosperity and continued good health. It also indicates a general upturn in both domestic and financial matters and prosperity in business. The larger the bottle and the lighter the colour of the drink, the stronger will be the potential for success.

*A **bottle of perfume*** This foretells a happy married life.

*A **broken bottle*** This warns of financial loss. If there are several broken bottles, the loss will be proportionately large.

Being given a bottle Irrespective of its size and colour, as long as the bottle contains some liquid, this dream indicates that you have every reason to depend on your friends. If the bottle is empty, however, you should take it as a warning to be careful not to depend too heavily on those around you.

See also **Drinking, Wine**

Boxes Although the size and colour of the box rarely has a prophetic significance, boxes in dreams can have a number of interpretations depending on the circumstances of the dream.

*A **closed box*** Whether metal or wooden, a closed box indicates you will have difficulties in making decisions.

*An **open box*** If the box is open and contains anything, take it as encouragement to go ahead with your plans as they will be successful. If the box is empty, it signifies false promises or unpleasant news.

Opening a box This dream underlines your strong ability to persevere. If you find difficulty in opening the box, you may be faced with temporary hardships, but if you manage to open it, you can be assured of at least partial success in your endeavours.

Being given a box Regardless of the size of the box, this indicates that you will experience good luck in all aspects of your life.

Breaking open a box This dream indicates that you are likely to uncover a secret of some kind and that you will overcome any conspiracies or bad feeling against you. It also means that you will make new friends who will be far more trustworthy than those you have argued with.

Boys In a dream, boys symbolise good health and a new beginning in life. They can indicate high energy levels, recovery from illness and a sudden change in life which is likely to be for the better.

Boys playing A favourable sign, indicating an end to a difficult period. It also means an end to domestic and financial problems.

Boys quarrelling This dream is a direct warning to stop your extravagant ways immediately and to listen to the advice of those around you, especially those older than you. You have not been using your logic to solve simple problems and may have been acting rashly. If one or more of the boys appears to be injured, it strengthens the dream and means that you must take a serious look at how you are behaving in your day-to-day life. *See also* **Children**

Bread Regardless of the size or colour of the loaf, seeing bread in a dream often signals the end of a period of unhappiness or difficulty and should be taken as a sign of moral encouragement. The quantity of bread reflects the degree of happiness you will receive. Stale bread signifies a failure on your part in the past to utilise the opportunities which were open to you.

Buying bread This indicates that there are possibilities for financial prosperity ahead of you, perhaps even more than you had anticipated.

Distributing bread to the needy This dream underlines your philanthropic nature.

Eating bread Such a dream means that you will enjoy a long and healthy life. If you are ill, you are likely to recover quickly.

Being given bread If the bread is given to you by an elderly person, it denotes an unexpected inheritance. If it is given to you by a young person of the same sex, it indicates that you will find a way out of a difficult financial situation. If you are given bread by a young person of the opposite sex, you are likely to have a happy married life.

Making bread This dream indicates that you will always be able to make a good living and will be willing and able to help others.

Throwing away bread Such a dream denotes domestic and financial problems, and heated arguments that may even end violently. It also forebodes sad news in the family.

Breasts A woman's breasts symbolise strength, vitality, courage and the ability to overcome hardships.

Seeing a woman's breasts If the woman is naked, you will continue to enjoy good health. If you have a minor illness, you will recover quickly.

Touching a woman's breasts This is an unmistakable sign of courage gathering within you to challenge the hardships and difficulties of your life. If the breasts are swollen with milk, it is a definite sign of swift success to one of your projects.

A woman breastfeeding Seeing a woman breastfeeding her baby is a good sign denoting a gradual strengthening of your will-power.

A wounded breast This is a harbinger of a temporary period of setbacks, although they will not have any acute or lasting effect on your health or general situation.

A man develops breasts This means you have the potential within you to embark on a more constructive project in life. Your success, however, will depend on your perseverance.

Bribes Bribing or being bribed in a dream symbolises an unsure present and a difficult future.

Witnessing an act of bribery If the act does not concern your affairs and you do not recognise the people, it is an open warning to be more serious in your search for a better life. If you recognise either of the people involved, it underlines the fact that you are in a precarious position. If the transaction involves you, you are likely to become involved in legal matters.

Accepting a bribe This means that you are as yet undecided and unable to guide your own destiny.

Offering a bribe Whether the person accepts your bribe or not, such a dream indicates a very difficult period ahead for you. Try to be more practical.

See also **Money**

Bricklayers Hard work, perseverance and hope are indicated by a bricklayer in a dream. It also reflects traditional values and indicates ability, good health and a hatred of greed.

Being a bricklayer Good health is indicated by this dream, as well as general happiness and contentment. If you are working with others, it means you will finally begin to face the challenges of life with a positive outlook. It also means that you will find a way out of a period of stagnation.

Receiving something from a bricklayer You should return to traditional moral values.

Seeing a bricklayer Seeing a bricklayer who is not working is a sign of hope for those in distress. Seeing him at work is a signal to initiate plans for a constructive life.

Talking with a bricklayer Avoid greed or ruthlessness.

Bridges A bridge in a dream is an indication of favourable opportunities. Whether of metal, stone or concrete, it indicates that there is potential within you just waiting to be exploited. It is also a signal to disregard those who appear to discourage you. If the span of the bridge is short, you may attain your aspirations within a short time, while a long bridge, although still promising success, indicates that it will take some time to achieve. If the bridge is broken or damaged, it signifies that you will have temporary problems in pursuing your goals.

Crossing a bridge This is a good sign, an assurance that you are on the right path. If you are in a car or riding a bicycle, the time it takes to achieve your goals will be short.

A bridge being demolished Your activities, perhaps even illegal activities, are leading you into trouble. If the bridge is close to you, you have done a lot of damage already and should expect to suffer the consequences. If the bridge is some way away, you still have time to rectify the situation by a change of behaviour.

Brooms Dreams involving brooms can be interpreted in very different ways, so must be viewed with caution. Some people feel that seeing a broom in a dream indicates a sudden change for the better and encourages you to be optimistic and patient. Others, however, believe that it indicates that there are hard times ahead.

Sweeping with a broom Such a dream means that the problems you are having to face are making you nervous. If you appear to have finished sweeping a place to your satisfaction, it denotes the end of an unhappy period.

Brothers A brother of any age in a dream symbolises support and courage. If you do not actually have a brother, believing that you do in a dream is highly auspicious, indicating that you will have the strength and energy to bring your plans to successful fruition. The dream also indicates that you have good friends who will stand by you unwaveringly.

Seeing your brother If you see one of your own brothers in a dream, it indicates that a controversial period of your life is coming to an end. It also means good news if you are waiting for an answer to an important question.

Brown *see* **Colours**

Bulls A grazing bull indicates that you are heading for prosperity. If you are near the animal in a peaceful atmosphere, this should encourage you to go ahead with your plans.
Feeding a bull This is a sign of good health, or recovery if you have been ill.
A dead bull This underlines your nervous and hesitant behaviour.
Riding a bull You are likely to experience a modest financial gain.

Burials Burials in a dream symbolise burying the past and therefore new beginnings. They also symbolise the possibilities for solving all your problems. If you know the person who is to be buried, it means you will very soon start on a new phase in your life. If you do not know them, it means someone you will meet soon will play an important role in shaping your life.
Attending a burial If you are involved with the ceremony in any way, it indicates that your marriage will be a happy one, or that you will soon find a new and loving partner.
Assisting at a burial This dream foretells good news. If you see anyone you recognise, it means that you will get help from a member of your family.
See also **Cemeteries, Funerals, Graves**

Burning The significance of burning in a dream depends on what is burning and your own reaction to it.
Seeing an unidentified object in flames If the item is inanimate, such as wood, property or any other object, it signifies a general loss due to your own recklessness.
Seeing a person burning This dream signifies an end of one particular cycle in life and therefore heralds a new one. Such a dream asks you to approach your life with a totally different outlook from the one you have had up to this point.
Seeing yourself burning Even if you feel the heat of the flames, this does not indicate any form of loss or grave situation for you. In fact, it indicates very strongly that you will experience an imminent change for the better.
See also **Fire**

Buses *see* **Coaches**

Butchers A butcher in a dream symbolises intolerance, anger, revenge and fraud. It indicates that you are too temperamental and are gradually losing what little tolerance you do possess.
Being a butcher This is an inauspicious dream, foretelling quarrels that may end in legal problems. It can also mean endless litigation and disputes with acquaintances, which may create a revengeful attitude within you. If you are actually selling meat, it denotes a more friendly attitude, but if you are chopping meat, you must be careful not to indulge in fraudulent behaviour.
Talking with a butcher You will have some heated arguments at home that may end in deep misunderstandings. If you are married, such a dream is likely to be followed by arguments with your partner.
See also **Meat**

Butter Butter symbolises the easing of difficulties and is therefore a dream often experienced by those whose fortunes are about to change for the better.
Butter on a plate Butter on a plate presages the imminent end to most of your worries.
Butter wrapped in paper or cloth This signifies hope. If you are entangled in legal problems, you will find a way out through compromise. For those who are separated, there is hope of a reconciliation.
Eating butter You have entered a new phase in your life without realising it and it will be to your advantage. For those awaiting a decision, expect promotion, good news in business or even an unexpected inheritance.

Buttons Buttons in a dream are symbolic of a person's character.
Buttons lying around This dream means that it is about time you began thinking seriously about your future.
Buying buttons You are well aware of the hardships facing you.
Buttons missing from your clothes If one or two buttons are missing, it means that your present situation may not improve for some time, but if you have lost all your buttons, it indicates that you must radically alter your goals, as they are too idealistic. You must approach life in a more logical and realistic way if you are to succeed.
Sewing on buttons This dream means you are making efforts to undo the harm that you have yourself created. If you have

already sewn on the buttons, it is a good sign that better days are in store, since you have now changed your attitude.

Buying Buying something in your dream indicates a healthy financial situation.

Buying food You are likely to be on the right track in your life. However, if you are standing around in a food shop not doing anything constructive, then this could be what you are doing with your life: idly passing the time without any positive plans. If you want to buy something but are unable to pay for it, you could be depending too much on false hopes.

Buying a house If you are discussing the possibility of buying a house in your dream while in real life this would be totally out of the question, it means that things will change considerably to your advantage. If you own a house, it means that you will become better off because of your own hard work. If you appear to have already bought a house, it means simply that you will have enough to meet your needs.

Buying something small This means that your financial situation will be such that you will be able to lead a modest life.

Buying a little snack This denotes a strong desire to resist temptations to enter into any illegal dealings.

Buying a ticket Whether the ticket is for a train, bus or aeroplane, it presages a new and fruitful beginning in a place a long way from your present home.

See also **Money**

C

Cabbages Cabbages symbolise good health, a happy married life, good friends and a successful job.
Cooking cabbage Your family will be supportive.
Buying a cabbage Success is on the horizon.
Eating cabbage This dream suggests you will enjoy good health.
Giving or receiving a cabbage You will have a successful love affair or marriage.

Cages Dreaming about cages has been called a prisoner's dream. It is a symbol of restrictions and constraints on your way of life and your ability to achieve your goals. It also means that you may be losing the ability to fulfil your potential through conspiracy or jealousy. A cage is a place where one is stifled, strangulated and even, finally, destroyed. If you dream of a cage, you should find ways to change your way of life drastically, otherwise the consequences could be dire. If you are the main wage-earner in your family, you will have difficult times ahead. Concentrate on developing a more positive attitude to life.
Seeing yourself in a cage This dream signifies a serious warning and a last-minute signal to reconsider the way you run your life. If you have been responsible for illegal or immoral actions, you will be made to atone for your actions.
See also **Prison**

Camels Seeing a camel in a dream reminds you to continue your hard work as you will be successful.
A camel feeding Prepare for a time of temporary hardship.
Being attacked by a camel You are likely to experience a short-lived disappointment at work.
Riding a camel Travel is indicated.
A dead camel You will be able to overcome any problems you may have.

Candles Usually, only people with a religious faith or strong spiritual dimension dream of candles and it is rare for anyone who is greedy or malicious to have this dream.

A lighted candle or candles This signifies that your prayers will finally be answered. You will find a solution to your problems and an end to present unhappiness. For the helpless or homeless, there is light at the end of the tunnel. If there are several lighted candles, the significance of the dream is strengthened.

Lighting a candle Your prayers have been answered, even if you were not immediately aware that this had come about. If you have been praying for good health, an improvement in your financial or domestic situation or any other reasonable request, you have attained what you asked for. If, after lighting the candle, you continue to hold it in your hand, you are aware of the advantages you have received but want to continue to thank and praise your god for the benefits you have received.

An unlit candle This is a reminder to repay your debts to your God. Perhaps you have been forgetful in acknowledging your spiritual debts, although it does not necessarily mean that you are ungrateful. If you then light the candle in your dream, it implies that you are reaffirming your spiritual beliefs.

Buying candles You will soon receive good news, possibly of the improving health of a family member of friend. This dream can also mean that domestic problems will be resolved to everyone's satisfaction.

Cannons *see* **Weapons**

Canoes A canoe in a dream is an indication of how you are likely to progress in the things you want to achieve. You must expect a determined struggle if you want to put your plans into effect.

Travelling in a canoe Although you have had an encouraging start, you still have to work hard to make your way up the ladder. If the water is choppy, your progress will be difficult. If the water is calm, you will achieve your goals more easily. If someone is paddling with you in the canoe, you will arrive at your goal more quickly.

See also **Boats**

Cards This is an inauspicious dream. A deck of playing cards or a single card suggests poor financial standing. Debtors and those who are reckless with money are likely to have this dream.

Playing a card game If you are playing with a deck of cards, either alone or with others, it indicates financial losses.

Being given a deck of playing cards Be cautious, as some of those around you who say they are your friends are not to be trusted. Make your own decisions and take the advice of a trusted friend or member of your family. Don't make any rash decisions.

Carpenters Since a carpenter can create useful objects out of blocks of wood, dreaming of a carpenter signifies an imminent transformation in your life for the better. It is a sign that things are on the right track towards general prosperity.

Being a carpenter If you target your efforts towards your goal, you will be successful. You may even expect a change in your profession or lifestyle.

Arguing with a carpenter This often indicates that you are being obstinate about changing your ways and suggests that you are showing a lack of interest in making efforts to improve your life, although you have all the necessary means at your disposal.

Chatting with a carpenter You are eager to accept expert advice and this will be to your advantage.

Carpets If you see a hand-made carpet or rug, the significance of the dream is in the fact that its beauty and quality is the result of patience, skill and hard work. Lazy, dishonest or corrupt individuals rarely, if ever, dream of such things. If the carpet is very beautiful, it underlines your patience in working to achieve your ambitions and the fact that you will not use underhand means. Even if you are experiencing hardships at present, remain honest and straightforward in your dealings and you will succeed in the end.

Weaving a carpet This is a wonderful dream, which shows that you will succeed and will be rewarded for your modest and honest approach. Success may not be startling, but it is quite close.

Walking on a carpet The rewards for all your hard work are on the way. You will experience the respect of your friends or colleagues and their confidence in you, which is well founded, will increase.

Being given a carpet Your friends and family are honest and dependable and will help you out when you most need them. They trust you and will be happy to support you.

Carriages, horse-drawn If you see a horse-drawn vehicle, this can have both a good and a bad meaning, depending on the carriage itself and where you see it.

A carriage with black horses This is an inauspicious sign, because of its funereal associations. It could mean bad news, illness, or even death.

A carriage with white horses On the other hand, this is an auspicious sign indicating a celebration of some kind. This may be due to a marriage, recovery from illness, success in business or a promotion.

A carriage without horses A bad sign, this dream warns you to be more practical and realistic in life. It also means that you could be heading for misunderstandings with your partner, friends or family. Try to be a little more thoughtful in your dealings with others.

Carrots Hardship and financial problems are indicated by dreaming of carrots.

Buying carrots Problems related to your home are indicated.

Eating carrots If you continue to be lazy, you will find your circumstances will deteriorate. If you are drinking carrot juice, your difficulties are likely to be financial.

Picking carrots You will have to work very hard just to attain your basic needs.

Cars A car or any other similar vehicle in a dream is an auspicious sign: you will find that you move forward and improve your life for the better, in the same way that the car moves forward on its wheels.

Buying a car You have finally decided to make the most of your potential to move ahead in life. Go for it.

Driving a car You are searching for prosperity and improvement in life. If you are alone, you are independent and determined to make it on your own.

Being driven in a car This is a wonderful dream, signifying that you will have help and support in your endeavours. If you are driving slowly, you may take some time to achieve your goals but you will get there. If you are driving fast, then you will make speedier progress.

Selling your car This is an unfavourable dream as it underlines your discontent with your present employment. You may suffer

a temporary, or even medium-term, period of financial instability and domestic upheaval. Your wheel of life may not stop indefinitely, but it is likely to receive a considerable setback. Search within yourself to find the strength to change your negative attitude and you will be able to battle against any unfortunate circumstances that come your way.
See also **Driving, Travelling**

Carts *see* **Wheelbarrows**

Castles *see* **Mansions**

Cats Cats in dreams usually indicate problems of some kind.
A sleeping cat Deceit and conspiracies by people you have trusted are indicated.
A cat scratches you This may indicate marital or relationship problems.
A cat bites you There may be problems relating to your children.
A friendly cat Arguments or misunderstandings with your family may be likely.
A dead cat You are about to see an end to a severe problem which has been worrying you.

Caves A cave is a primitive home and therefore dreaming of caves signifies a return to primitive behaviour in your home, resulting in unhappiness and even a complete breakdown in relationships, separation or divorce. In all cases, it indicates that you need to be more considerate. If you have a quick temper, you need to be more thoughtful and less inclined to fly off the handle. If you have been acting recklessly, it is a sign that you should be less extravagant and plan more carefully for the future.
Being in a cave You must change your attitude and behaviour otherwise you are in for a rough time, especially at home. If there are people or animals in the cave with you, other people will also suffer from your behaviour.

Celebrations Celebrations in a dream indicate future prosperity and happiness.
A religious celebration You have a spiritual approach to life and will soon reap the rewards of your prayers for an improvement in family relations.

A non-religious celebration Even if the celebration does not directly concern you, this dream is a harbinger of good health and financial prosperity. For those suffering financial problems, solutions are at hand; for the sick, you will soon recover.

Joining in a celebration You are aware that things have been changing for the better recently. These changes will continue if you carry on in the same way.

Cemeteries Although often considered eerie places in real life, this is not so in a dream. A cemetery or graveyard is considered to mark the end of one cycle of life but the beginning of another in a better place.

Standing in a cemetery Good things will happen soon. There is every indication that you will be successful in your business and domestic affairs, even to the point of a total change in your lifestyle. Anyone who has been bearing a grudge against you will ultimately compromise to your satisfaction.

Sleeping in a cemetery This denotes absolute comfort; you have overcome any problems and are ready to implement life changes.

See also **Burials, Graves**

Certificates The nature of the certificate changes the significance of the dream.

Being awarded a certificate Since a certificate usually indicates a positive achievement, this dream means that your hard work and honesty will be rewarded sooner or later. If the certificate is for sporting achievement, you will enjoy continued good health. If the certificate is for educational achievement, you will continue to be happy and enjoy a well-balanced attitude to life.

Presenting a certificate You have a considerate nature and like to help others, and will be rewarded for your benevolence.

A death certificate Health problems are indicated.

Chains Not surprisingly, chains in dreams suggest abnormal behaviour. A chain is an object of bondage, suffering, hardships and limitations. Whether you see a chain or touch it or use it on a person or animal, it signifies that you have at best an indifferent and at worst a callous and ruthless attitude to others.

Being chained up This suggests you will ultimately be judged for your arrogance, ruthlessness or even crimes, if you have committed any. Those who disagree with you will be successful in bringing you down.

Chaining a person or animal This dream should make you realise that you have been brutal and violent in temperament and behaviour. Take steps to change your attitude.

Chairs A chair of any kind is a sign of authority, negotiation or even legal procedures. There are different interpretations depending on the circumstances of the dream.
Sitting on a chair lecturing a group sitting on the ground This indicates an important public position from which you will exert authority.
Sitting around a table with others You are negotiating a business deal that could be favourable to you.
Empty chairs around a table Take steps to compromise and sort out any disagreements otherwise they are likely to end in legal proceedings which will not turn out to your advantage.

Charity This dream signifies health, wealth and happiness.
Giving to charity This is always a good dream indicating prosperity and happiness. If your finances are already healthy, dreaming of giving money to charity indicates that you will prosper even further. If you are planning to embark on a business trip, it will be successful. If you are planning to marry, you will be happy with your partner.
Receiving charity Receiving charity does not mean that you will suffer misfortune but rather that you are on the verge of becoming successful. Improvements are on the way.

Châteaux *see* **Mansions**

Cheating Dreaming about cheating or being cheated is considered an undesirable dream.
Cheating others This suggests that you are independent and do not like to depend on others or have them depend on you. You can also be fickle and weak in decision-making situations.
Cheating at gambling You make things difficult for yourself in your daily life by being disorganised. You could also be acting hypocritically, risking the distrust of others and a breakdown in your domestic affairs, perhaps even a break-up with your spouse or partner.
Being cheated This does not necessarily signify that you are an innocent party. Most authorities agreed that it implies that you

will lose any advantages you may have gained by unfair or illegal means.

Cheese Cheese is a staple food and dreaming of it is an indicator of good health and prospects for a pleasant way of life.
Buying cheese You want to continue in your current way of life without social or financial upheavals. You are likely to be happy in your personal relationships and will achieve your ambitions.
Eating cheese This is an assurance that you will maintain your good health and standard of living; it also emphasises that you are not over-ambitious or greedy but are happy with a relatively simple life.
Offering cheese to others Your ambitions are on the verge of fruition and your business and financial matters will prosper.

Chemists *see* **Pharmacies**

Chess Playing chess in a dream is an indication of optimism, despite present difficulties. Since the game is an attempt to overcome an opponent, the dream indicates that you are putting serious efforts into overcoming any difficulties you may be experiencing.
Playing chess You consistently use a positive approach to problem-solving. If you win the game, you are on the way to achieving your ambitions, even though you may have encountered difficulties on the way. If you lose, it does not mean that you will be defeated in life, but it does indicate that you have to continue to struggle patiently against the odds.
Being given a chess set You will have faithful friends around you, and you will always use honest means to get what you want.
See also **Board games**

Chickens Chickens in dreams generally indicate rewards.
A chicken feeding Your hard work will be rewarded, even if you have to wait a little while to achieve your goals.
A hen with chicks You are likely to receive a sudden and unexpected financial gain.
A dead chicken You may experience a temporary setback.
See also **Cockerels**

Children Children in a dream are usually a sign of joy and warmth and can also indicate a successful married life and financial prosperity.

Children giving flowers, fruits or sweets This dream promises a promotion or unexpected success in business.

Children quarrelling Although this is rare in a dream, it could indicate some domestic problems, although these will only be temporary.

Chimneys Chimneys in dreams are concerned with productivity.

A smoking chimney Any chimney emitting smoke is a sign of honesty, hard work and perseverance. Regardless of the type of chimney, this emphasises that you have an honest and simple approach to life which you should try to maintain as it will be rewarding in the long run.

A smokeless chimney This dream indicates a loss of productive activity and is a warning not to be tempted to follow a dubious route towards making a living. It may appear promising but it will damage more than your reputation.

Churches *see* **Religious buildings**

Cigarettes Virtually everyone agrees that dreaming of a cigarette, cigar or tobacco-burning pipe has a negative connotation: that of wasting physical or mental energy. You need to revise your unrealistic or illogical goals as pursuing them is wasting time and energy.

Being offered a cigarette Be cautious about those around you and do not follow over-optimistic advice. It will lead to more worries and even perhaps legal proceedings against you.

Lighting a cigarette This dream can indicate a setback in business or domestic affairs through your own irresponsibility. It can also indicate that you have a nervous disposition.

Smoking a cigarette Something in your life, whether business or personal, is causing you difficulties. You have consciously chosen a hopeless attitude rather than fight to overcome your problems.

Cigars *see* **Cigarettes**

Circles A circle is a symbol of completion and perfection of a cycle in life and is considered a favourable sign in a dream.
Drawing a circle This is a good omen and denotes your determination to achieve your goals, however difficult and challenging they may appear.
Looking at a circle you have just drawn A wonderful dream, this signifies that you have the potential to achieve your ambitions. Activate your potential with determination and you will succeed.

Cities A city is a symbol of work, expansion, prosperity and development.
Finding yourself in a city Go ahead with your business plans and your ambitions will materialise. You will be supported by friends and colleagues.
Finding yourself in a ruined city This is a warning of impending financial problems and even legal proceedings against you. However, if you see friendly people there with you, the effects of the problems will be less severe.
Leaving a city You may be discouraged by a work-based situation. If you reflect on the significance of what is happening, you will be able to view it more philosophically.

Cleaning Cleaning a place or an object generally signifies getting rid of obstacles in your life. The interpretation varies depending on the circumstances in the dream.
Cleaning a house This is a sign that you are nearing the completion of a business deal and that you will be successful both in that and in other aspects of your professional life. If you are being helped in the dream, you have a trustworthy business partner.
Cleaning the bathroom This is a sign of good health and recovery from illness. It also indicates a balanced and creative mind.
Cleaning the kitchen You can expect the arrival of guests or a reunion with old friends.

Climbing Climbing a hill in a dream indicates that you have the will to overcome difficulties and strive to achieve perfection.
Climbing a hill or a mountain Your strong determination to overcome difficulties means that you will put up with hardships

if necessary. Since climbing a mountain is associated with risk in life, in a dream it also indicates that you may have to make some sacrifices to achieve your goal, although you will do so by honest means. It is also a dream that indicates that you have considerable patience. If you are being helped by another person, you will have a smoother path to attaining your goal.

Climbing a ladder This is a sign of imminent success in your projects and indicates the full realisation of any dreams and ambitions that you may have.

Climbing a steep slope The path to your objective is not without risks, but with care and planning you will overcome them.

Climbing a tree If you are climbing with difficulty or are afraid, this dream signifies your refusal to accept the facts of life and you are trying to escape from the inevitable. If you fall, it is a strong warning to change your ways. If you climb the tree without much effort, you will achieve your ambitions.

See also **Hills, Ladders, Mountains, Rocks, Trees, Walls**

Clocks This dream interpretation applies to any timepiece. A clock in your dream suggests that time is on your side and signifies a major success in business or finance.

A large, broken clock You need to move fast if you are going to avoid difficulties and setbacks, but success can be achieved.

Buying a clock You are too worried about what is happening around you and may be acting impatiently. Slow down and take stock of the situation.

Receiving a clock as a gift You will be helped by your own hard work and also by your family to achieve your ambitions. The significance is the same if you receive a watch, but is less pronounced.

Clothes

Putting on your clothes This means that you will finally begin to move towards a better time in your life. Although progress may be slow, take note of positive signs that should encourage you to continue your progress.

Removing your clothes Deliberately removing your clothes emphasises your strong wish to remain traditional and simple. It also means that you attach great importance to spiritual and moral values. However, if you simply find yourself naked in a dream, that indicates hard times ahead.

Receiving clothes as a gift This can indicate promotion, recovery from illness, reconciliation with friends or family, or unexpected guests, depending on your circumstances in life.
Buying clothes This is an auspicious dream signifying your determination to start a new life all over again. It also means that you will travel extensively before finally settling on a place to live.
See also **Nakedness, Undressing**

Clouds Clouds can be interpreted as either good or bad depending on their colour and the situation in which you see them in your dream.
Cloudy skies If the sky is full of rain clouds, it foretells a breakthrough for the better. However, if the dark clouds are patchy, it suggestions some emotional problems.
Clouds partially covering the sun This is an indication that you must not give up hope. It should encourage you to be patient, as your hard work will be rewarded in the long run, albeit modestly.
White clouds Good news, better health, improved personal relationships and even an improvement in your financial situation are predicted.
See also **Rain, Skies**

Clowns A clown in a dream symbolises transience and even falsehood. It is therefore usually a dream experienced by people who are unsure of themselves, fickle or lacking in self-confidence. Take the dream as a warning telling you to be serious and constructive in your approach to life and more focused on achieving your ambitions.
Yourself as a clown An inauspicious dream, this can indicate imminent financial crises and even legal proceedings against you arising out of your own irresponsibility. Pay closer attention to your affairs and overhaul your future plans in detail.

Coaches If you are travelling in a coach or bus, it signifies a long but fruitful journey towards achieving a particular goal in life. The journey may be actual or metaphorical, but you will continue in your efforts towards prosperity. Don't be discouraged by minor difficulties; whether in personal or business matters, you are likely to succeed. A fast-moving coach indicates that you

will realise your ambitions more quickly than if the coach is travelling slowly. Time is on your side and you will find prosperity and happiness. Be patient and honest and you will find what you seek.
See also **Travelling**

Coal Depending on the circumstances in the dream, coal can have a good or a bad significance.
Holding a piece of coal If the coal is wet, it suggests that you have a long way to go before you get what you want. If the coal is dry, you are holding the power to achieve.
A hot coal This warns you not to be extravagant otherwise your behaviour could lead you into problems.
A heap of coal Worries and family arguments may be forthcoming. If you are involved in a long-standing dispute, it could also indicate separation or divorce.
See also **Fire**

Coats Coats in dreams usually symbolise support and comfort.
Giving a coat to someone If you recognise the person to whom you are giving the coat, the friendship between you will be strong. If you do not recognise them, you will accidentally come across a new and useful friend.
Being given a coat This indicates that timely help will come your way.
Wearing a coat This signifies comfort and also means that you will live a modest and respectable life.
A woollen coat This type of coat indicates comfort, honour and respect in life.
See also **Clothes, Jackets**

Cobwebs Different interpretations of spiders' webs in a dream can be given depending on the circumstances.
A large cobweb covering an entrance If the web is intact, it suggests that you are a prisoner of your own narrow-mindedness and lack of understanding.
A cobweb with a spider on or near it You will experience continued problems from those around you who call themselves your friends. Be more cautious in your dealings with people.
A torn cobweb If there is no spider on the cobweb or the spider is dead, you will soon recognise openings towards an

improvement in your life. Be determined and act independently, or seek out trustworthy friends and colleagues.

A cobweb being spun This is a strong warning of impending problems, although they may still be some way ahead. Consider the consequences of what you are doing, otherwise you will run into difficulties.

Tearing down a cobweb You have the potential to control your own destiny. You will be able to shake off troublesome acquaintances and can look forward to a sudden change for the better in your health or your domestic or business affairs.

See also **Spiders**

Cockerels A cockerel signifies anger and unnecessary difficulties caused by rashness.

A cockerel crowing If it is perched, be careful not to create misunderstandings between friends or colleagues that may become serious. If it crows while on the ground, a lovers' quarrel is indicated.

A dead cockerel You should soon come to the end of a difficult period.

See also **Chickens**

Cockroaches Seeing or touching a cockroach in a dream is an indication of something wrong in your attitude towards life.

Cockroaches on the ground Ill-health is indicated.

Flying cockroaches You are likely to have a difficult journey in the near future.

Cockroaches on a wall There are likely to be arguments in your family.

A dead cockroach Your present problems are coming to an end.

Killing a cockroach You are likely to change your ways for the better.

Coffee Dreaming of coffee is usually linked with business and financial prosperity.

Drinking coffee Seeing yourself drinking coffee with friends means that your hard work to succeed in business will be rewarded over the next few months. If you are alone, be encouraged to go ahead with planned business deals, which may involve a change of location.

Being served coffee You are about to embark on a major business deal, with the co-operation of your business associates, and it will conclude successfully and to your benefit. If you are looking for a job, something suitable is not far away. If you are already in work, expect a promotion or new proposals.

Coffee beans Although not highly auspicious, coffee beans in dream do not necessarily mean bad news. They denote an immature attitude which could lead to temporary setbacks if you do not take a wider and more realistic viewpoint.

Coffins Coffins in dreams symbolise the end of one cycle of life, but the beginning of another. They may indicate radical changes for the better in your lifestyle, such as financial recovery and improved health.
A well-made coffin If the coffin is in a good state of repair, this strengthens the significance of the dream. However, if the coffin is damaged in any way, you will experience delays in reaching your goals, probably because of your own lack of determination.
An empty coffin So-called friends will break their promises.
Yourself lying in a coffin This is a good dream. Those looking for marriage will find a partner; if you are experiencing financial difficulties, a breakthrough is on the horizon; if you are looking for a job, you will be successful. Misunderstandings between family or friends will be resolved.
See also **Burial, Corpses, Death, Funerals, Hearses**

Coins A single coin denotes the beginning of a period in which you will use your imagination and creativity to add meaning to your life.
Coins lying around you There are better times to come as you make progress in your job.
Being given a coin or coins This is a warning of difficult times on the way, due to your own lack of judgement in domestic or financial affairs. Your attitude to life is too easy-going and irresponsible. Take sound advice and adopt a more cautious and responsible philosophy.
See also **Money, Silver**

Cold Feeling cold in a dream is suggestive of anxiety, often about the way you have behaved towards family or friends. Although you

49

may not mean to harm others, you are clinging to unrealistic values and not being honest with yourself. Review your attitude and find a more sensible viewpoint.

Cold limbs Feeling cold in the limbs, particularly the hands or feet, suggests your anxiety is becoming intolerable. Find the time and the means to relax.

Colours Colours emphasise and reflect positive and negative forces as well as human emotions. When you are considering the implications of colours in a dream, think about where they appear: on houses, trees, birds, clothes and so on.

Black Black symbolises absolute recklessness and disregard of life by taking risks without considering or caring about the consequences. If black predominates in a dream, take care to follow a more rational and reasonable approach.

Dark blue Dark blue reflects a mysterious and undependable character. If you see this colour on anyone you recognise, beware of them. If you do not know the person, it should act as a general warning not to be too trustworthy. Seen on a building or wall, it suggests that you should practise restraint on your fiery temper. On a vehicle, a bird or any moving object, it indicates violence or revenge. If someone appears to paint this colour on you, you are likely to be deceived by someone you thought was your friend. Be more realistic and responsible.

Light blue Light blue reflects the vast expanse of space, the sky, and infinite possibilities for your spiritual development. It also emphasises the high degree of importance you attach to moral values. You set yourself high standards, but you are likely to achieve them.

Dark brown This colour reflects irrelevance, indecision and an inability to face difficulties. It is a dream for the lazy and lethargic and is rarely seen by those who are practical and energetic. This colour in a dream reminds the dreamer that you have to act today to achieve anything tomorrow.

Light brown Unlike dark brown, light brown reminds dreamers that they hold within themselves the potential to achieve their ambitions. It is therefore rarely seen in a dream by those who act maliciously. Forge ahead with your plans and you will succeed.

Green Green in a dream is a general indication not to have illusions about others as they can be harmful to you. It can indicate that you are harbouring suspicions that your partner, or someone close to you, is not being honest with you. If that is the case and you recognise the person in your dream, be cautious in your dealings with them as you could be proved right. On the other hand, if you recognise the person in your dream, and, in real life you have no such suspicions and their behaviour is open and friendly, you can be reassured that any fears are groundless.

Orange Orange or saffron-colour indicates a person who has a strong spiritual presence. If you have been discouraged in your search for spiritual enlightenment, have patience and it will be rewarded. If you find yourself dressed in orange, it underlines your wish to shun materialism in favour of spiritualism.

Red This colour reflects a fiery temper, anger at injustice and the urge to strike back at detractors. Anyone experiencing such violent emotions who dreams of red should take it as a warning to exercise restraint, otherwise the consequences could be tragic. Revenge or retaliation are not advisable.

White The significance of this colour in a dream depends on who sees it. Most people who see white in a dream can expect a continued period of tranquillity as this colour reflects their calm and friendly temperament. However, if seen by someone who is contemplating revenge, it emphasises a violent temperament and negative consequences unless they take a calmer attitude and initiate a change of course.

Yellow Anyone dreaming of yellow is likely to be at a stage in their life where they have no positive goals and are drifting along in a state of general fatigue. In this case, it is essential for the dreamer to take steps towards improving their own feelings of self-worth and self-confidence so that they can begin to move forward in life.

Comets The sighting of a comet used to be associated with major catastrophes affecting the Earth, such as floods, volcanic eruptions, earthquakes or floods. It is still often regarded as an indication that you will experience some unexpected unhappiness, perhaps a family argument, separation or divorce, serious difficulties at work or a major business loss.

Cooking This is a good sign in a dream as cooking symbolises nourishment, health and a modest life.
Cooking for yourself If you are alone, you are likely to experience temporary loneliness.

Cooking for others This dream emphasises your selfless character and reflects your general desire to help others.

Someone else cooking Had it not been for the good example set by your friends, your uncontrolled temper would have landed you in trouble. However, help from family members will help you realise your modest aims in life.

See also **Kitchens**

Corpses A corpse in a dream symbolises impending difficulties in several spheres of your life. This could mean domestic misunderstandings, a sudden break in a close friendship, an impending quarrel or a worsening of illness.

A woman's corpse This denotes either an illness, hardship or even death for a female. For married men, it could mean an unpleasant separation or divorce.

Yourself as a corpse This is a strong warning to change your life as you have envisaged the potential results of your irresponsible behaviour, whether actual or metaphorical.

A dead body lying on the ground Help is at hand from an unexpected quarter.

A body floating on water You will experience a sudden breakthrough, which will improve your circumstances.

See also **Coffins, Death, Funerals, Skeletons**

Cots *see* **Cradles**

Countryside A beautiful country scene in a dream is often attributed to the positive results of your hard work.

Being in the countryside If green and beautiful, this dream foretells success in business, employment and domestic affairs. If barren, it indicates a defeat and even a retreat from life.

Leaving the countryside You may have a sudden setback in business, which can be overcome through serious and wise consideration.

Desolate countryside Good news and a fresh start are on the horizon.

Courts of law A court of law in a dream can indicate dishonesty in a person, although if the court is friendly, it can symbolise financial gain, perhaps through inheritance.

Being confronted in a court This indicates an inner dishonesty for which you will be answerable sooner or later.

Having a pleasant conversation in a court You are likely to benefit from a windfall from an unexpected source, perhaps an inheritance.

Being ordered to present yourself in a court This dream is a precursor of a legal proceeding against you. If you appear to have been arrested and are being led into court, it means that you will be convicted. If you go to the court voluntarily, however, it suggests that you will be able to bring the case to an end through negotiation and compromise.

See also **Innocence, Judges, Lawyers**

Courtyards In dreams, courtyards indicate achievement through effort.

Standing in a courtyard You are satisfied with your achievements, however modest, even though you have undergone considerable stress in order to get where you are. Reconciliation is indicated if you have been experiencing difficulties in a personal relationship.

Yourself with friends in a courtyard There will be a happy ending to family arguments. If refreshments are being served, it indicates that you have overcome many of your difficulties.

Workers working in a courtyard This is a good dream suggesting that your friends will do whatever they can to help you. You will not be left alone.

Cradles Cradles symbolise planning and the future.

An empty cradle Beware of unrealistic plans and try to be more practical. You could also encounter problems if you make empty promises.

A cradle with a baby A good sign, this dream promises ways to get on in life. It also suggests that family and friends will support you through the bad times.

A sleeping baby in a cradle This is a sign of calm and tranquillity.

A cradle with a crying baby You will experience difficulties when you arrive at your goals.

See also **Babies**

Crickets *see* **Grasshoppers**

Crime Crime in a dream symbolises an uncomfortable period and that the dreamer may be tempted to indulge in criminal activity in real life as well as in the dream.
Committing a crime yourself It seems that you would consider doing the same thing in real life. Think hard about the choices you have to make; illegal activity can never be justified.
Seeing others committing a crime This is a strong warning that legal proceedings may be started against you if you go ahead with the criminal intentions you have been considering.

Criminals Seeing criminals of any kind in a dream symbolises reckless behaviour and a general reluctance to try to develop the potential of your life.
Being a criminal This dream underlines your criminal intentions. If you are robbing, attacking or burning a property, it signifies that evil has taken over your character, either in fact or in intention. Take steps to change your ways.
Criminals who do not harm you Take this dream as a warning that some disaster awaits you unless you move fast enough to prevent it.
Criminals attacking you or your property If you appear helpless, it suggests the results of past activities will prove costly for you in one way or another. If you confront them or frighten them away, a last-minute change in your lifestyle will prevent a catastrophic situation for you and your family.
See also **Arrests, Courts of law**

Crocodiles A crocodile or an alligator in a dream symbolises deceit, misunderstandings and unfaithfulness in love.
Crocodiles on land Personal relationships are likely to be badly affected.
Crocodiles in the water You are likely to be affected by jealousy or back-biting in professional areas of your life.
Being chased by a crocodile Petty arguments among those close to you could lead to serious misunderstandings unless you handle them carefully. However, if the reptile passes you by, the tense period will be short and will end satisfactorily for all concerned.
A crocodile in a zoo Friends will help you to cope with any problems you encounter.

Crosses A cross, in whatever form, design or material, is a symbol of spiritual calm and blessing. It also signifies a simple and uneventful social life.
A small cross If it is the type you would hang round your neck, it is a reminder that you must remember the spiritual values in life.
A large cross You should alter your greedy and grasping lifestyle.
Receiving a cross as a gift If it is given by a religious figure, it denotes satisfaction in life and a wish to exchange your material wealth for spiritual enlightenment. Your family is likely to have a simple but rewarding life.

Crowns A crown in a dream symbolises prestige, position and respect. You may be about to gain a promotion in your job or a breakthrough in business affairs. It also indicates a happily married life, whether or not you are already married.
Crowning yourself Not a good dream; this signifies that you have an egotistical approach to life and can be uncompromising or even dishonest.
Others crowning you Other people's confidence in you will increase and you may also be appointed to a position of responsibility.

Crows A single crow symbolises longevity and good health.
A flock of crows You will ultimately receive your just rewards.
A crow in flight You are likely to embark on a short journey.
Crows quarrelling over a carcass There are deep misunderstandings within your family, although the problems will be resolved.
A dead crow You may face a long period of difficulties coupled with bad health.

Crutches Crutches in dreams symbolise overcoming difficulties.
Walking with crutches You will have a long and tiring journey towards achieving your goals but, since crutches are a means of helping you to walk, you will receive help from an unexpected source.
Being given a pair of crutches Your minor problems will soon be at an end and you can look forward to better times, especially in business and financial affairs.

Crying Depending on who is crying, this dream can have different interpretations.

Crying with sadness This is a good omen suggesting an end to domestic worries. If you are experiencing a difficult time in personal relationships, you can expect a resolution to your problems. If you actually wake yourself up with the intensity of your crying in the dream, this indicates success in your financial affairs or in love.

A child crying This dream suggests an unexpected marriage or a happy married life, depending on your circumstances. Seeing your own children crying means that you will have a happy family life.

An old person crying An old woman crying suggests marital problems; an old man crying suggests sudden death in the family.

Your parents crying They will have a carefree life.

Your partner crying You are likely to have a good relationship.

Cucumbers Cucumbers symbolise good health, perseverance and honesty.

Buying cucumbers You are honest and keen to persevere in whatever you take on.

Eating cucumbers This dream suggests you will enjoy good health or will recover from illness if you have not been well.

Picking cucumbers You have a strong conscience.

Cups Depending on the circumstances, this dream can have a number of meanings.

A beautiful cup If the cup is full, the dream denotes that you are in the prime of your life and will enjoy both a peaceful and a happy existence for some time. If the cup is empty, it signifies that you are too concerned with material things and either have emotional worries or need to pay more attention to the things that really matter.

A broken cup Your friends are likely to desert you when you need them most. Try to avoid depending too much on other people.

Breaking a cup You can let your temper get the better of you and would be wise to practise restraint. You may also experience some financial loss.

Being offered a cup containing a hot drink This is a
wonderful dream signifying sudden good news which will
change your life for the better.
See also **Drinking**

Curtains A large curtain dividing two rooms is often associated
with secrecy. Such a dream suggests that members of your
family are hiding something from you.
Opening curtains This indicates that you will expose and
ultimately triumph over any unjustified criticisms levelled
against you by those pretending to be your friends. It also
signifies the completion of a business deal or personal project.

Cuts
Cutting yourself accidentally This dream has little or no
significance.
Being cut accidentally If there is only a little blood from the
wound, this dream could mean that you are very careless, and so
are some of your friends. If there is a lot of blood flowing from
the cut, the dream can be considered organic (see page 9) and
therefore of no significance.
Being cut intentionally Beware of those claiming to be your
friends because they may be involved in a conspiracy against you
in matters of the heart.
Cutting someone intentionally You are becoming rash and
nervous and may be heading for misunderstandings at home.
See also **Daggers, Knives, Swords, Wounds**

D

Daggers A dagger symbolises deceit and ungratefulness. It also indicates that you have enemies whom you have not yet recognised, some of whom may be masquerading as friends.

A dagger on a table or raised surface Be on your guard against those who profess to be your friends.

A dagger on the floor You have already made several enemies and it is time to disassociate yourself from them.

Someone else holding a dagger If the dagger is in the hands of someone who does not threaten you, try to avoid entering into an argument. The negative effects of the dream will be lessened if the dagger is in its sheath.

Holding a dagger in your hand If you appear to threaten or intend to harm someone in your dream, this underlines your unreasonable behaviour and sharp temper. You need to adopt a calmer and more restrained attitude.

Being threatened with a dagger If you are being threatened by someone you know, your progress will be hindered by your own faults. If you do not recognise the person, a short period of difficulty will be followed by a marked improvement.

Dancing Dancing in a dream symbolises joy and good news.

Dancing with a partner Look out for good news.

Dancing alone Either you are satisfied with your own performance in life, or some help or a gift that will add to your happiness is already on its way.

People dancing If you appear to be watching others dancing, it means that there is every reason for a modest celebration since, after a long period of waiting, you will finally reap the rewards of your hard work.

Being invited to a dance This suggests good news from family members or a new employment proposal.

See also **Celebrations**

Danger Danger in a dream symbolises uneasiness and anxiety.

Seeing yourself in danger Your acute anxiety over a certain development appears to have taken over all your energies. If you dislike a person and you see them as threatening to kill you in your dream, this does not mean they actually pose a danger to you. If that person tells you they will take their revenge on you, it indicates that you can be relieved of your anxieties if you take time to gain a better understanding of the circumstances surrounding you.

Seeing danger pass you by A good sign, this indicates moral and physical recovery. You will gradually overcome your hardships through perseverance and concerted effort.

See also **Accidents, Falling, Suffocation**

Darkness Darkness in a dream is usually attributed to the general ups and downs of life, although some other interpretations can be made depending on the circumstances.

Finding yourself suddenly in absolute darkness You appear to have been kept unaware of events confronting you, either through the jealousy or conspiracy of others, or perhaps because you have not been sufficiently careful to weigh up the true consequences of your actions. Only a determined approach to your activities can help get you out of a difficult situation.

Walking from sunlight into darkness You are losing your courage at the first sight of a simple challenge. You have no one but yourself to blame for your unhappiness and it will last until you muster the determination to face your problems and deal with them.

Walking from darkness into sunlight You will experience further prosperity in life and your hard work will be rewarded.

Dates Dates symbolise spiritual values and an indifference to materialism.

Buying dates This underlines your strong intention to develop your spiritual values.

Eating dates Hard work and honesty are indicated by this dream.

Picking dates This indicates a successful journey.

Selling dates You have an intense desire to avoid materialism.

Daughters In most cases, a daughter in a dream is a sign of joy and an end to domestic problems, but it can have the opposite interpretation depending on the daughter's behaviour.

Your daughter looking happy This is a generally favourable sign for the whole family.

Your daughter working or playing If she is singing, dancing, writing, weaving, walking or swimming in the dream, it indicates a change in the household, usually for the better.

Your daughter complaining or unhappy There are family problems that need to be sorted out fairly soon.

Your daughter sick or crying There is likely to be a family argument.

Your daughter scolding you You have not been the best of parents and could face an embarrassing situation very soon. If, however, she attacks you verbally or physically, it is a sign of her ungrateful nature.

Your daughter introducing her future husband This is a good sign of financial prosperity, unless you dream of the same situation repeatedly, in which case it indicates that your daughter has difficult times ahead of her. If she is adult and bitterly attacks her present or future husband, it means there will be major setbacks in the family.

Your daughter is pregnant If she is happy and in a stable relationship, it is a sign of good times, but if she is unhappy and is not in a loving relationship, it could indicate deep conflict within the family.

Deafness Being deaf in a dream symbolises continued laziness and irresponsibility.

Being deaf You are indifferent to those around you and to the mundane things of everyday life. Be more practical and realistic otherwise you will accumulate further problems, which will be difficult to solve.

Speaking to a deaf person You should take great care to avoid rash decisions, especially when you are selecting a partner in life, a business partner, a friend or even a profession.

Death Dreaming of death is a dream of opposite meaning as it indicates a long, healthy and prosperous life. It can also mean a new life with new friends.

Your own death The setbacks you have recently experienced have brought you to the point of deciding that you are ready to move on to new horizons. Since you have already given this much consideration and you are ready to meet the inevitable challenges, seeing your own death is a sign that things will go as you have planned. Use whatever means you can to muster the courage and confidence to move forward.

Witnessing someone's death If you know the deceased and if they are, in reality, sick, they are likely to recover. If you do not recognise the person, your general situation will improve, perhaps through the intervention of an acquaintance or friend. *See also* **Coffins, Corpses, Graves, Killing**

Deception Whether you deceive or are deceived in a dream, it means you should be wary of trusting those around you.
Being deceived If you do not trust your partner in life and you dream of being frightened by their deception, be cautious in your dealings with them.
Being deceitful You are harbouring distrust and dislike for someone, or perhaps more than one person, which will cause you mental anxiety. If someone in the dream encourages you to deceive a person, and you know that person, it is a warning to avoid their company. However, if you do not recognise them, it means that you are in danger of using methods that will not only lose you respect, but could land you in trouble.

Deer Deer in dreams have a variety of meanings.
A running deer You may hesitate in making decisions, especially if the animal appears frightened.
A deer approaching you You are likely to encounter success.
A dead deer You may have untrustworthy friends.
A herd of deer There is likely to be a gradual rise in your social and financial status.

Demolition Seeing a building being demolished in a dream is a general indication of difficulty.
Demolition of your house If it is on your instructions, you can look forward to a new life coupled with spiritual advantages. If the house is being demolished against your wishes, however, your own carelessness will lead to losses and considerable unhappiness.
Demolition of a bridge You have done considerable damage to your reputation through your immoral, perhaps even illegal, activities. If the bridge is near to you, expect to suffer the consequences of your actions. If it is some way off, you still have time to rectify the situation if you act soon to change your behaviour.
See also **Destruction**

Deserts A desert in a dream symbolises bitterness, hardships, sadness and loneliness. There are only a few specific instances in which a dream of a desert is favourable.

Being in a desert If you appear suddenly in the middle of a desert, it means that your partner will be the chief source of your mental anguish. If you are not already married, such a dream warns you to take great care in your choice of a partner. If you can see an oasis, it indicates that your own sensible behaviour will defuse the situation and you will be able to restore harmony. If you appear tired, hungry and thirsty, it means that you are on the verge of giving up hope. However, since the shifting sands symbolise temporary hardships, you should persevere as your determination and genuine efforts will set the wheels of progress in motion again soon.

Eating in a desert You are likely to succeed through your own efforts and should be wary of relying on false promises.

Seeing someone in a desert If you see your partner, it indicates financial loss. If you see friends, it is a sure sign of consolation. *See also* **Oases**

Desks Depending on your situation, this dream can have a good or bad interpretation. A desk covered with documents, papers or books signifies that times will change for the better with a little effort. If the desk is empty, it denotes a period marked by unemployment and domestic problems.

Sitting idly behind a desk Such a dream warns of an impending financial loss, and even bankruptcy if proper care is not taken in your financial affairs.

Buying a desk This means that you are contemplating doing the right thing at the right time. Go ahead.

Selling or breaking up a desk This dream reflects a deep and depressive mood. Try to find and resolve the cause and begin to think more positively about life.

Working at a desk Your determination to improve your life through hard work and patience will pay off, but be cautious of any haphazard moves and do not enter into any new business ventures until you are assured that your past efforts have been successful.

Destruction Destruction of a place, property or surroundings in a dream has different meanings depending on the circumstances. In all cases, the interpretations relate to seeing the building in ruins or being pulled down.

Destruction of a centre of education Your educational career will end through your own fault.

Destruction of a hospital You have been misusing your body through alcohol, drug or other abuse.

Destruction of a house If it is your own house, it suggests general loss due to your own inability to manage your affairs. If you do not recognise the house, it denotes an unhealthy atmosphere at work.

Destruction of a prison This indicates the end of hardships and a favourable end to any legal problems.

Destruction of a recreational centre You may suffer ill-health because of your own carelessness. Take steps to remedy the situation.

Destruction of a centre of vice or corruption You will see an end to your grief or difficulties and reap the rewards for your honesty and hard work over the next few months.

Destruction of a village An ominous cycle in your life is coming to an end.

Destruction of a place of worship Whatever the place of worship, this dream indicates a tense period of anger, legal problems, arguments and even violence. It may be a reflection of the deep anger within you occasioned by your not achieving success as you had expected. If you see people trying to restore the destroyed building, it means that last-minute effort, coupled with help, would greatly ease whatever problems you are currently undergoing. Try to control your emotions and direct your energies into a positive channel.

See also **Demolition**

Devils A devil in any form symbolises unfavourable temptations. If the devil appears to be near you, it indicates that you are experiencing a strong temptation to join in an immoral or illegal activity and that, if you take that path, it will bring you unbearable unhappiness.

Talking with a devil If you exchange friendly conversation with a devil, it denotes possible danger through accident, drowning or violence.

Confronting a devil Consider it a good omen if you confront a devil, standing up to him either verbally or physically, since it

means that you will be able to overcome the temptation to commit evil acts.
See also **Hell**

Diamonds Diamonds in a dream symbolise false illusions, illness and loss. Try to be more realistic in your approach to life.
Wearing diamonds If you wear diamonds around your neck or on a ring or if you are holding them, it indicates illness or a violent confrontation with a member of your family.
Finding a diamond You are heading for a business loss. Plan out all your business activities with particular care.
Being given diamonds If you receive a gift of a diamond from anyone other than your spouse or partner, it indicates serious misunderstandings, which could lead to a very ugly situation. Choose your words carefully when you discuss important issues. If you are given diamonds by your spouse, you may not be able to trust them as much as you thought. If you are given diamonds by your son or daughter, it is a good sign of promising financial prospects.

Digging Interpretations of digging in a dream vary depending on the circumstances.
Digging for water An unfavourable dream for those in business, this can indicate financial loss. For others, it could mean alienation from other members of the family.
Digging to plant a tree A good dream, this underlines your determination to prosper through honest means. You may also have strong religious convictions.
Digging for precious metals You are still living in a world of illusions. Be more practical in your outlook.
Digging a grave This is a good sign, promising a new beginning in life.
Seeing others digging This dream indicates that your circumstances are likely to improve, especially if there is a house in the area.
Seeing others digging a grave Accept the wise advice of friends and family.

Dirt Dirt of any kind symbolises a general setback.
A dirty body If it is your body, you should be more careful, prudent and active; your style of life may be too carefree for

your own good. If your partner's body is dirty, it could mean that they have been deceiving you, or that they have not been living up to your expectations.

Dirty clothes If your clothes are dirty, you may not have been making the required effort in life, but have instead been leaving everything to fate. However, if both your clothes and your body are dirty, it could signal a long period of illness, perhaps even ending in tragedy. If you see your children in dirty clothes, it indicates that you have not taken your parental responsibilities seriously.

Divorce Dreaming about divorce is only significant for those who are married or in a long-term relationship, and the meaning of the dream varies.

Discussing divorce with your wife (men) You are likely to suffer a long period of unhappiness caused by your own unreasonable behaviour. If you have planned this action in real life and regularly dream about seeking a divorce, you may have jumped to some wrong conclusions. Try to discuss matters reasonably and find ways of relaxing. If you ask your wife for a divorce in a dream and she consents, she is honest and a reconciliation is possible. If she argues, however, the prospects are less good.

Discussing divorce with your husband (women) Whether you are seeking a divorce or your husband has asked for one, this dream indicates that although relations with your husband may go through a difficult time, you will eventually be reconciled.

Doctors Since a doctor is a symbol of treatment and cure, the presence of a doctor in a dream indicates good health and prosperity. Seeing one or more doctors in a dream indicates that friends will be happy to help you when you turn to them for assistance.

Meeting or speaking with a doctor Whether or not you are ill in the dream, you are on the way to recovery from a minor illness in real life.

Being visited by a doctor This dream is a harbinger of prosperity and modest financial gain. If the doctor praises you, it means that things will improve for you.

See also **Hospitals, Illness, Nurses**

Dogs A dog symbolises friendship, faithfulness and truth.

Your own dog You are likely to receive some valuable help from a friend.

A strange dog A new friendship is on the horizon, although if the dog is menacing, it means that you could experience some misunderstandings with friends.

Friendly dogs surrounding you Good news is on the way.

Dead or injured dogs This signifies your compassionate and honest nature, although it can also suggest blighted hope. If you attempt to hurt or kill a dog, it certainly indicates arguments or misunderstandings, possibly within the family.

See also **Hounds**

Dolls Dolls symbolise falsehood and deceit.

Dolls in a room There may be conspiracies around that are working against you.

Someone holding a doll Do not trust people without being sure of their motives.

Yourself with a doll You are living in a fool's paradise. Be more realistic in your outlook. If you see your partner with a doll or if they give one to you as a gift, be cautious as you may not be able to trust their motives.

Buying a doll You are likely to make some friends soon who will turn out to be not only useless but dangerous.

Throwing away or destroying a doll You are determined to abandon your unrealistic attitudes and be more serious and focused.

Donkeys If you see a donkey near you in a dream, it means you will receive valuable advice and even practical support.

Riding a donkey Your wise and cautious nature is likely to work to your benefit in the long run.

A donkey attacking you You may not have been sufficiently careful in your planning.

A dead donkey You have been unrealistic.

Doorbells The sight or sound of a doorbell symbolises joy and happiness. You may receive a visit from a much-liked family member or a good friend, or it may indicate good news.

Ringing a doorbell As long as the bell is not your own, this means that you will soon meet someone who will greatly influence your lifestyle.

Doors A door in a dream symbolises opportunities for success.

An open door You will have unlimited opportunities to try your luck, whether in business, employment or education.

A partially closed door You should try to make some effort to create opportunities. Things may look hopeless, but you do have the potential to do so.

A closed door Advancement may be a hard struggle but you will get there in the end.

A broken door You have missed an opportunity.

An old door You have been indifferent to the chances you have had in life.

Installing a door This is a wonderful dream signifying a good period on the way for you if you continue to work towards your goals.

Doves A dove in a dream is a symbol of your honest and moral way of life, and if it is flying, it means you will do well on your own.

A pair of doves A happy married life is indicated.

A flock of doves in flight You offer support and help for those less fortunate than you.

A dead dove This is a warning that you should cherish your spiritual leanings. If you are very close to the dove it signifies that you will attain inner peace and calm.

Drinking There are various interpretations of drinking in a dream.

Drinking water This is a sign of continued good health, or a quick recovery if you are unwell. Drinking contaminated or muddy water signifies an impending illness or domestic problems.

Drinking water from a fountain Regardless of the quality of the water, this dream indicates financial prosperity and domestic happiness.

Being offered water The person offering you the water is loving and trustworthy.

Drinking wine or other intoxicating drinks If you are drinking with friends, you will soon achieve your modest ambitions. If you are drinking alone, it forebodes some loss and domestic problems. Whatever the circumstances, drinking alcohol in a dream is a warning that you should move quickly to re-plan your activities otherwise you will face a devastating period.

See also **Coffee, Tea, Wine**

Driving A dream about driving symbolises the state of your emotions, and you can judge this by the way you are driving. **Driving a vehicle** If you appear to be well in control of the vehicle, it means you are at the helm of your destiny and need no outside interference. If you are also driving slowly, you are happy with the speed of your progress, but if you are driving too fast, you are trying to reach your goals too quickly and are likely to be disappointed with the eventual results. **Being driven** You are likely to receive some assistance that will be greatly to your advantage. However, if you are being driven forcefully or against your will, it indicates severe worries about work or a domestic situation that could turn ugly. If you have recently had an argument with your partner or a colleague at work, try to exercise calm and restraint. *See also* **Cars, Travelling**

Drowning If you experience drowning in a dream, it indicates that you are likely to experience difficulties in your life. **Being in danger of drowning** You are likely to experience difficulties and worries as a result of your past behaviour. **Actually drowning** The feeling of submersion is parallelled by the feeling you are likely to experience of being overcome by problems, mainly as a result of your own behaviour. If you have been argumentative, try to seek a resolution. If you have been gambling or abusing alcohol or drugs, take positive steps to face and overcome your addiction. **Someone trying to drown you** If you recognise the person, take care in your relationships with them, especially if it is your partner or a member of your family. *See also* **Danger, Swimming**

Drugs Since drugs in any form are considered agents that gradually and progressively destroy a human being's mind and body, any sign of abusing drugs in a dream indicates the possibility of severe mental or physical problems and should be taken as a warning that you should change your behaviour immediately. If you have been using drugs in real life, such a dream indicates serious consequences if you continue to use them. **Being offered drugs** If you accept them, it indicates that you are unaware of the difficulties surrounding you and this could have negative consequences. If you refuse them, there is every chance that you will get out of the difficulties in which you find yourself.

People using drugs You are having serious doubts about your circumstances and what your next move should be.

Ducks Ducks in dreams symbolise happiness.

Ducks swimming There is a happy atmosphere in your home.

Ducks in flight A long and prosperous journey is in prospect. A single duck in flight suggests uncertainty in your projects.

A dead duck You may have a misunderstanding with your partner.

Dumbness If an image of being unable to speak appears in your dream, it infers that you have a weakness in dealing with a person or people who are giving you a hard time.

Being dumb If you have recently had an argument or confrontation with someone and felt that their opinions were unjust but you were unable to voice your point of view, this dream indicates that someone will give you the support you need to overcome your problem. If you have been involved in a confrontation, even a legal dispute, and you secretly know that you are in the wrong, however, the dream indicates that you will be truer to your conscience if you do not try to claim innocence.

Your partner suffering dumbness This could indicate that you are not being totally honest with your partner; perhaps an open conversation about matters important to you should be attempted.

Seeing a dumb person If you recognise the person, the dream means that you need to summon up the courage to face the difficulties that life has presented to you. If you do not recognise them, it means that you may not be able to find that courage.

Quarrelling with a dumb person This indicates that you are having difficulty understanding the circumstances surrounding you.

Dung Dreaming of dung is considered favourable since it is a fertiliser and can help you achieve better things.

Being surrounded by dung Things will change for the better in your life. You may get a promotion, business should thrive, your finances or your health could improve.

Spreading dung on a field You will soon see positive results for all your hard work, and an acknowledgement that success only comes through determination and hard work.

Dung being thrown at you or falling into a heap of dung You are likely to receive a gift of some kind, or a general improvement in your finances.

Duvets *see* **Blankets**

E

Eagles An eagle symbolises high aspirations and a tendency to
dominate.
An eagle circling in the sky Your goals may be over-ambitious.
An eagle flying in a particular direction You have a very
strong ambition, which is likely to succeed.
An eagle sitting on a cliff or a tree This dream emphasises
your domineering nature.
A dead eagle You should reassess your over-ambitious plans.

Earrings These symbolise a dreamy nature combined with
difficulties.
Golden earrings Whether you are wearing or holding them or
they are lying in front of you, these suggest that you will have
to achieve much if you want to realise your ambitions.
Silver earrings Any of the difficulties you are likely to face may
be intensified. If they contain diamonds or other precious stones,
you should take a more practical approach to life.
Buying earrings Be careful that your behaviour is not
extravagant or you will run into financial problems.
See also **Jewellery**

Earthquakes Seeing or being told of an earthquake is not a
favourable dream since it symbolises loss, sudden change and
unhappiness. If the earthquake has devastated a village or town,
you are likely to encounter problems from a number of
directions. They may include difficulties at work or at home,
poor health or arguments with your partner.
Standing in the middle of a devastated region You will have
to face unbearable problems over the next few weeks and you
will find these very stressful. Try to remain calm and take a
reasoned approach to sorting them out as they will be short-
lived. If you are planning to move, try to postpone the
completion date for a few weeks.

Eating Eating in a dream is a symbol of good health and happiness,
although this can depend slightly on what you are eating.
Eating in company If you are with friends and the atmosphere
is amicable, it is a sign of business success; if you are with your

parents, it indicates hard work rewarded; if you are with your partner, it is a sign of continuing good health.

Eating alone If you see yourself eating alone and feeling unhappy, you can expect arguments with your partner, perhaps through your own fault. Try to be more honest in your dealings with those close to you.

See also **Kitchens, Restaurants**

Eggs Dreaming of birds' eggs is generally a good omen, while dreaming of reptiles' eggs is not.

Birds' eggs Hens' eggs suggest that your cautious plans are likely to be rewarded. Eggs from ducks or geese herald an end to family arguments and even to financial problems. Turkey eggs denote slight inconsistencies in your life that will demand some careful thought from you. Pigeon eggs imply that you have an inflated ego and are inclined to be lazy.

Broken birds' eggs Stress or nervousness is preventing you from reaching your full potential. Address the cause and you will find things are likely to improve. If the eggs are crushed, this means that you must move quickly if you are to prevent a general loss in your life.

Rotten birds' eggs You have insincere friends. Trust only those you are sure of, as there are others who are not as honest as they may appear.

Recently hatched eggs and birds A particularly rare dream, this generally indicates health, wealth and happiness, although if the chicks are dead, it can be a sign of forthcoming ill-health.

Reptiles' eggs Intact reptiles' eggs in a dream are considered a bad omen indicating a future crossed by arguments, illness and even violence.

Crushed or broken reptiles' eggs Since the eggs are damaged, the problems you will encounter will either be less severe or be quickly dealt with.

Recently hatched reptiles' eggs and young You must take great care to avoid potentially dangerous circumstances as you are likely to be surrounded by difficulties. If there are dead reptiles near the eggs you will survive the difficulties you face.

See also **Nests**

Elephants An elephant close to you suggests that you are wise and sensible.

Riding an elephant Success will come to you through honest hard work.

A trumpeting elephant If the elephant is raising its trunk or trumpeting, you will achieve your ambitions in time.

Speaking to an elephant You have a strong moral sense, which you will maintain whatever the cost.

See also **Ivory**

Embalming A symbol of continuity, seeing an animal or human in an embalmed state in a dream is generally a favourable indication.

An embalmed human being If the embalmed person is of the opposite sex and you are married or in a relationship, this indicates that your relationship is strong and will continue to be so. If you see someone you recognise, you are likely to continue to be successful in business.

An embalmed animal or bird This symbol in a dream can indicate a contented home life. A bird often indicates a financial breakthrough.

Something being embalmed If it is an animal, health or finances are likely to improve. If it is a bird, you will experience a sudden change which is likely to be for the better. If it is a person, your life will be long and healthy.

Embraces Embracing someone in a dream denotes your ability to forget the past. If you recognise the person and you have actually argued with them, happily embracing them in a dream is a sign that you will resolve your differences.

Embracing your business partner You are embarking on a good business venture.

Embracing your children You will soon be reconciled with your partner or a member of your family with whom you have disagreed. If you have not argued, it symbolises that the strong bond of friendship you share will continue.

Embracing a stranger You will soon resolve a hostile relationship with someone who has been causing you problems.

Embracing someone you hate If, in the dream, you are aware that they are still your enemy, then you are likely to have a hypocritical attitude to life that could cause you problems.

Embers *see* **Ash, Fire**

Employers These can have either favourable or unfavourable connotations. If you see someone you know in this role, it could mean a promotion, better employment prospects or a new job if you have been unemployed.
Yourself as an employer You will eventually run your own business, even if only in a modest way.

Enemies Seeing an enemy in a dream signifies nervousness and angry behaviour. If you see a former enemy with whom you have now resolved your differences, it indicates that you will continue to make mistakes through hasty decisions. If you see someone whom you imagine to be your enemy, it means you are inclined to be unrealistic. Seeing a person who hates you means you will be unhappy at home.
Being reconciled with an enemy If you manage to reconcile your differences in the dream, it is a good sign that you will achieve the same measure of success in life.
Quarrelling with an enemy The bitterness you experience in the dream will continue into your life.

Excrement This symbolises an end to hardship and suffering. Whether it is in a lavatory or on the ground, this dream denotes an end to your social problems or to the stress you have been experiencing. No matter how difficult it appears to achieve your goals, you will do so in the end.
Yourself passing excrement Petty problems will quickly be resolved. If you have defecated in your clothes, the problems you have experienced have been to do with the family and you were unaware that it was your own perception that exaggerated the degree of the problem.
Eating excrement Sudden help is likely to come from the most unexpected quarter and it will improve your circumstances for the better.

Execution There are several ways of interpreting these dreams, depending on the particular details.
Witnessing an execution If you recognise the victim as an innocent person, it means your activities, whether business or social, will take a down-turn. If you do not recognise the person, it indicates a period of uncertainty. If you see a criminal being executed, it indicates that things will come right for you.

Being executed If you feel that you have already been executed, it means a new beginning in life that will be much better than you would have expected. If you appear to be ready for an execution, it means that you will meet new friends and the association will be financially rewarding.

See also **Death, Gallows, Hanging**

Exile If you dream about being exiled or sent away from the people and places you love, it reflects your unhappiness and frustration.

Yourself in exile You are likely to change your location and the results may not be to your advantage.

Your family or friends are exiled You must be more rational and practical in your approach to life.

Eyes If you appear to focus on the eyes of a person in a dream, you are searching for a more meaningful life. Different types of eyes will offer different interpretations.

Angry or aggressive eyes Your choices are not appreciated by others.

Red or swollen eyes You will soon face a temporary period of setbacks or ill-health.

Losing one or both eyes This dream signifies potential loss, perhaps within the family. It is especially likely to be a young person.

See also **Blindness**

F

Faces Depending on the type of face seen, several interpretations can be given of this dream.

Your own face If your face appears to be normal, it means that you will be moving into a more meaningful stage in your life. If you appear sad, then you will have difficulties and challenges to face. If you are happy, smiling or laughing, it means that even if you encounter difficulties in life, luck will take a hand in making sure you get through them.

A face you recognise If it is smiling, it denotes a sudden development for the better. If the face is angry, it indicates a short period of uneasiness.

Factories A factory symbolises hard work, success and satisfaction. Seeing a factory indicates that your hard work will reap rewards and that you are doing well in your job.

A smoking factory chimney You may receive a promotion or better job offer.

Being in a factory Such a dream promises a fulfilling social life and underlines your desire to be self-sufficient.

Working in a factory A wonderful dream foretelling success, albeit perhaps only modest, in all your activities.

Falling

Falling from a height You are experiencing anxiety, perhaps for no logical reason.

Fame A favourable dream symbolising opportunities and chances to realise at least some of your goals.

Being famous Even if the odds appear to be against you, you will be presented with an opportunity to change your life for the better. If you dream of any of your family members being famous, this also indicates good opportunities for you.

Famine Contrary to what you would expect, famine in a dream symbolises good things and happiness.

Being famine-stricken Better days are ahead and the resolution of particular problems of any kind which you are experiencing at the moment.

Seeing a famine-stricken region If you recognise the area, you will find prosperity there. If not, you will have to be patient in order to achieve your ambitions.
Famine in a particular region That area will be particularly prosperous.
See also **Hunger, Starvation**

Farms Farms in dreams symbolise prosperity, respect and continued friendship. If the farm appears well cared for and in good condition, it denotes prosperity through business or general good employment prospects. If you are unemployed, your prospects of finding a job or completing your qualifications are good.
Yourself on a farm If you are a writer, you will be successful. Those in business will be able to expand their businesses, although financial rewards may not be immediate. If you are a farm worker in real life, your dreams of owning your own farm will eventually be realised.
A farm on fire If you fail to take the practical opportunities open to you, then your efforts will not be rewarded and you will regret your lack of success. Channel your abilities and talents in a more practical way.
See also **Chickens, Hay, Pigs, Ploughing, Sheep**

Fathers Fathers in dreams are usually symbols of genuine love and affection.
Your father If you are suffering from ill-health or other difficulties in your life, seeing your father in a dream indicates that you will overcome your difficulties. If your father is alive, this dream underlines his considerable support for you. If he is dead and you are currently finding yourself in difficult circumstances, his appearance in a dream indicates that you should consider changing your course of action in order to ameliorate your circumstances. If your father is actually dead but in the dream you are unaware of this, it is a good sign if he appears friendly and happy as it indicates a time of calm ahead of you. If he appears unhappy, however, it can mean that you will have to be cautious in order to avoid unhappiness ahead. A dead father rarely speaks in a dream. If he gives you a gift, this indicates happiness and prosperity, although this may be some time in the future.

Feasts *see* **Banquets**

Feathers This dream can have opposite meanings depending on the details of the dream itself.

Black feathers You will not always understand the behaviour of those around you, whether family, friends or colleagues.

White feathers You are likely to have a simple life with few problems.

Buying or selling feathers This indicates dishonesty, either of those you have trusted, if you are buying feathers, or of yourself, if you are selling them.

Fighting Violence of any kind in a dream is usually associated with a fiery temper in the dreamer. You should try to control your temper and be less inclined to fly off the handle.

Fighting with your partner This dream indicates that you are having trouble understanding their way of thinking. Try to be more patient and see things from their point of view.

Fighting with a family member You are likely to gain financially in the near future and may inspire some envy in those around you.

Being injured while fighting This is not a good sign in that it implies that you will suffer some setbacks in life.

See also **Anger, Arguments**

Figs This fruit is usually associated with excellent health and possibly an inheritance.

A plate of figs You will enjoy a happy married life or an early marriage.

Eating figs This dream denotes excellent health.

Being offered figs You may come into some money.

Picking figs This dream indicates modest financial gain.

Rotten figs You are likely to experience family difficulties.

Finding If you dream of finding something valuable that you lost or mislaid, it indicates that you will recover from other losses you have experienced.

Fingernails Fingernails in dreams can have both a good and an unfavourable significance.

Tidy, well-kept fingernails You enjoy good health and mental stability.

Broken fingernails You are likely to suffer from ill-health and loneliness.

Cutting your fingernails You are about to enter a more prestigious and profitable profession.

Fingernail cuttings If you see but ignore these, you may be indifferent towards your own future. If you stamp on them or try to brush them away, you have an urge to do something constructive.

Fingers Different interpretations of fingers in dreams can be made depending on the details of the dream.

A finger pointing at you This is a warning to be more careful in your dealings. If the finger is pointed in a friendly manner, especially if the finger has a ring on it or if you recognise the person, it is a symbol of encouragement that things will turn out well for you. However, a finger pointing menacingly at you means that you should take seriously some threats that have been made to you.

A severed or bleeding finger If it is your own finger, this denotes arguments and misunderstandings with your family, or perhaps your in-laws if you are married. If you do not recognise the person, you are likely to be surrounded by jealousies, although these are unlikely to have any direct effect on you.
See also **Hands**

Fire Fire is often considered an organic dream (see page 9), but some significance can be interpreted.

Fire in a fireplace You will inspire warmth and affection in others and be happy in your married life.

Fire engulfing everything An ominous dream signifying a terrible development affecting your life in general, but especially your domestic and social affairs. Be cautious at work and postpone journeys, however short. If you see people fighting the blaze, there is a good chance that the intensity of the rough patch will be reduced. If the blaze dies out suddenly, however, the dream has no prophetic significance.

The hot embers of a fire Usually a dream for the honest, this is a reminder that hard work and perseverance finally pay off. Do not give up hope. There is good news for those who are sick or anyone who is experiencing difficulties in life.

The cold embers of a fire The difficult period you are experiencing – perhaps because of a misunderstanding in your

married life – will continue for some time but not indefinitely. Be patient and persevere and it will come out right in the end.
See also **Ash, Burning, Coal, Smoke**

Fish Fish in a dream generally symbolise prosperity and the realisation of ambitions.
A single fish in water This is a sign that you will be successful, especially if it looks at you.
Fish on land This indicates a degree of anger inside you, although this will pass.
Feeding fish Close friends or family will help you.
Touching fish You will achieve prosperity a long way from home.

Fishing This signifies a search for a new life. If you see yourself fishing in a dream, take it as an encouragement to continue your efforts. If you catch a fish, you are likely to achieve your ambitions.
Falling in the water while fishing Take more care in planning your actions, otherwise you will not be successful.

Flags A flag in a dream indicates honour. If you can identify the flag in your dream, it indicates promotion or success in achieving something you have been working for.
A foreign flag You will travel abroad.
A torn flag on the ground This indicates a period of difficulty.
Being given a flag People like you and approve of you.

Flames *see* **Burning, Candles, Fire**

Flies Seeing a fly in a dream is a suggestion that you have a greedy nature.
Flies on your body You may suffer from ill-health.
Flies on the ground You may have an inclination towards fraud or vice.

Floods and flooding Since floods are associated with destruction, if you see them in a dream, they usually indicate difficulties of either a financial or a business nature.
A flooded house Family misunderstandings are likely, which will create a difficult atmosphere for everyone.

Being engulfed by a flood You have only yourself to blame for the difficulties you are currently experiencing.

A flooded desert After a period of difficulty, this dream indicates that things will improve for you.

See also **Drowning, Rain, Rivers**

Flying A dream in which you feel as though you are flying is highly auspicious, indicating health and prosperity. The higher you are flying, the quicker your dreams will be realised.

Other people flying Go ahead with your plans. The rewards may not be startling, but you will certainly not lose out.

Flying objects see **Aeroplanes**

Football Playing soccer in a dream denotes your desire to have a good business partner or dependable friends.

Forests A forest symbolises the unknown.

A forest in the distance This indicates future uncertainty. Be practical and cautious and make sure that you make your own decisions and do not rely too heavily on others.

Being in a forest If you are alone but you know your way out, you will, in reality, find your way out of a difficult situation. If you are lost, you may well need professional help of some kind in order to straighten your affairs.

See also **Trees**

Forgiveness see **Innocence**

Fortified buildings Any kind of fort or fortified building is a symbol of power and determination. If it is in a good state of repair, it mirrors your strong will-power and determination. If it is in ruins or overgrown with vegetation, it is likely that your plans are uncertain.

Being inside a fort You will receive all the support you need and will be successful in your endeavours.

Seeing a fort overrun or occupied If the invaders around the fort are violent, there are people who are working against your best interests. If they appear to be friendly, be on the lookout for hypocrites who only claim to be on your side.

Fountains A fountain in a dream is a symbol of good health and also of life, if the water is clean.

A broken fountain Delays may cause you financial problems.

Drinking water from a fountain Your finances will be sound and you will be happy at home.

Foxes A fox symbolises a wily and unashamed nature. It can also suggest malice. If the fox is near you or threatens you, it suggests that some acquaintances are not being honest about their intentions towards you.

Chasing a fox away You can expect an undisturbed domestic life.

A dead fox Those who work against you will not succeed.

Killing a fox You will neutralise any malicious rumours spread about you.

Friends The presence of friends in a dream symbolises support. Only rarely do good friends speak in a dream.

Seeing old friends If the friends have been parted from you for some time, the dream means that you are lonely and believe you lack moral support.

Embracing a friend You will soon meet a new friend who may become very important to you.

Arguing with a friend The nervousness that exists between you and a former friend is underlined by this dream.

Frogs Frogs in dreams symbolise prosperity, health and happiness.

A swimming frog You will enjoy prosperity or a promotion.

A frog jumping into water There will be a decision in your favour.

Two or more frogs on land or in water You can look forward to good personal relationships and a happy marriage.

Mating frogs There will be an end to misunderstandings between friends.

A dead frog You have a careless and indifferent attitude to life.

Killing a frog Your approach to life is somewhat haphazard.

Frontiers A frontier or border of any kind indicates a need to move on to a new phase in your life. If you feel unable to cross, you will need to overcome difficulties mainly created by others. Be patient and quietly determined.

Crossing a frontier If you are considering a move, especially over a long distance, and you cross the border in your dream easily, it is a sign that the new location will suit you better than your present one.

Being stopped from crossing If you are prevented from crossing or subjected to embarrassing interrogations, then you ought to re-think any ideas you have for moving.

Being helped across a frontier by an official You may receive help from an unexpected quarter.

See also **Passports**

Funerals Funerals in dreams indicate the end of a phase of your life and the beginning of a new one, perhaps in another location. If you recognise the dead person in the funeral procession, that person will embark on a new and better stage in their life. If you do not recognise them and appear simply to be watching the funeral pass you by, your next project will be successful, whether you are starting a business, taking an examination or looking for a job.

A funeral pyre being lit This is a sure sign of a change of address.

Participating in your own funeral The end of a difficult period in your life and the start of a new phase, perhaps through a new job, a promotion or marriage.

See also **Burials, Cemeteries, Coffins, Corpses, Hearses, Mourning**

G

Gallows Gallows in dreams often denote a warning. If you doubt the motives of those around you, you will probably be proved right in the end, so proceed with caution. However, like other subjects to do with death, they may also indicate a new start.
People sitting near a gallows Even though you may have been warned against it, you are still far too arrogant for your own good.
Being led to the gallows Your miseries will end and you will start on a new and fruitful time in your life. If someone is accompanying you, you will make new and reliable friends. If you are frightened, you are worrying too much about things that are not important.
Escaping from the gallows If you have some dubious actions on your conscience, you will be forgiven.
Seeing someone led to the gallows Be wary of those closest to you as this is an indication that someone is trying to deceive you.
See also **Execution, Hanging**

Games *see* **Board games, Cards, Football, Hockey**

Gardeners A gardener in a dream symbolises peace, love, affection and sympathy.
A member of your family is a gardener The member of your family you see will enter one of the caring professions or will help those in distress in some way, perhaps through charitable work. If you recognise the dream person as a gardener in real life, it means that you are contemplating increasing the spiritual element in your life.
Being a gardener Your goals of serving others will be realised. If people praise you in the gardening dream, you will be supported; if they criticise you, you will have detractors but will continue your good work despite them.

Gardens Gardens in dreams are considered symbols of joy and happiness, especially happiness in marriage.
A well-kept garden You will be happily married.

An overgrown garden Your married life is likely to be equally unruly, usually as a result of misunderstandings, unless you are more careful to communicate and to listen to how others feel.
Walking with other people in a garden You are likely to find support from other people valuable in your life.

Garlic Garlic in a dream relates to good health and recovery from illness.

Gates A gate is a symbol of hope and is usually seen in dreams by those who have strong spiritual leanings.
A gate to a palace This generally indicates that your wish to serve others will be fulfilled. If the gate is open, the sacrifices you have made will be rewarded. If it is closed, others have tried to put obstacles in your path but they will not succeed.
An overgrown gate This indicates that you have not always taken life seriously. If you are trying to clear away the weeds and vegetation, you have been making efforts but you may have to work even harder.

Ghosts If you are frightened or threatened by a ghost or spirit in a dream but it then goes away, you can be reassured that the doubts you have about your present activities are unfounded. The dream has no significance if the dreamer is ill, stressed or frightened in any way.
A ghost gives you something You will be able to rise above your past, especially if it contains actions that you are not proud of.
A ghost speaks to you If the ghost asks something of you, you are likely to continue to experience difficulties.

Giants Anyone who is abnormally large in a dream can be considered a giant.
A friendly giant You will probably receive support from those around you.
An angry or threatening giant You may quarrel with your parents or your superiors at work.
A giant advising you You are likely to receive help from someone influential.
Being a giant If you feel as though you are physically towering over others around you, it means that a decision you have to make over the next few days will turn out very well for you.

Gifts

Receiving a gift Your hard work will be appreciated through either promotion or recognition of some kind.

Giraffes
A giraffe in a dream is an indication of a kind and unassuming nature.

A giraffe grazing Those around you will begin to understand you better.

Feeding a giraffe You have a helpful nature.

Several giraffes together either at rest or grazing You will achieve success after a struggle. If they are very close to you, it indicates success from unexpected quarters.

Girlfriends
This dream can have different interpretations depending on the circumstances.

Meeting your current girlfriend A dream about your current girlfriend generally denotes that you are likely to have a good future together, especially if she gives you a gift, as this underlines her love for you. However, if she is angry or aggressive towards you, it can have the opposite interpretation.

Meeting a former girlfriend If the atmosphere in the dream is emotional, you are still upset by the separation; you regret your decision if you were the cause of it, or miss her a great deal if she left you. If she is upset or crying, she may still have feelings towards you. If the atmosphere in the dream is normal and you know that in real life the girl forced the separation or holds a grudge against you, you can take this as an indication that she is not worth regretting, as she does not deserve your friendship.

Girls
Various interpretations can be made of dreaming about a girl, depending on your relationship with her. If you know the girl and she is smiling, friendly or affectionate, your general attitude of honesty and open dealing in life with be rewarded with success. If you do not know her and you find her beautiful, you may be embarking on a new love affair. If the girl appears untidy or is crying, angry or abusive, take care to show a little more understanding to your partner or to those around you, otherwise you may be in for some arguments and unnecessary misunderstandings.

A single woman becoming a girl Although it may not happen immediately, you will find happiness in marriage or a permanent relationship and it is likely that it will be with someone much younger than you.

A married woman becoming a girl For a happily married woman to dream this, it indicates that your health and financial status will continue to be good, or will improve if you have been ill or in financial difficulties recently. If your marriage is undergoing problems, things will turn out to your mutual satisfaction, either because you resolve your differences or you part on good terms.

Threatening a girl This is an ominous sign, which indicates that an accident may cause temporary health problems. Be a little more cautious than usual and try to avoid long journeys for a couple of weeks if you can.

Gloves Gloves symbolise carefulness and discreet behaviour. If you are wearing gloves in your dream, regardless of the weather or the type of gloves, you attach a great deal of importance to being particular and careful in your day-to-day activities.

Being given a pair of gloves If you are given a pair of gloves by someone you know, they are likely to have some positive feelings towards you. If you do not know them, be more careful in your dealings with other people as you may find an argumentative time ahead, either with your partner or with friends or colleagues. Try to relax a little more; you could be over-stressed.

Buying gloves This dream indicates your reticence in something you are dealing with at the moment.

Finding gloves You are likely to receive some good advice; consider it carefully.

Losing gloves You have a degree of irreverence towards life, which may not turn out for the best in the long term.

Holding a single glove You are feeling undecided about something and would do well to ask for some advice.

Goats A goat symbolises greed, a loss or sudden financial gain.

A goat grazing You could be becoming too greedy for your own good.

A single male goat with large horns If it is on high land, it means sudden financial gain; if it is on the same level as you, it is an indication of opportunities; if it is below you, there is potential for financial problems.

Gold *see* **Ingots, Jewellery**

Gorillas
  A gorilla in a cage This denotes impending unhappiness, possibly legal problems or unemployment.
  A gorilla in a forest Unless you make changes, you will have an unfruitful life.

Grain Any type of edible grain in a dream indicates happiness, prosperity and good health. If you are in a warehouse or a shop and see sacks of grain piled around you, this is a sign of abundance coming your way in some form. It could have a fairly literal meaning in that you can expect a good crop, a rise in your salary or a successful outcome to your practical endeavours. It could mean a reconciliation with someone, or a marriage.
  Grain thrown on the ground You are wasting opportunities by your reckless behaviour. You may not always be so lucky, so you would be well advised to be more considerate.
  Collecting grain from the ground You are trying to be more serious and responsible in your outlook, and you will find you benefit from the change of attitude.

Grapes Grapes usually symbolise success both in love and at work. They are also a sign of continued good health.
  Buying grapes A bad time is coming to an end.
  Drinking grape juice Your good health will continue.
  Eating grapes Success in love and a happy marriage are indicated by this dream.
  Picking grapes A prosperous period is beginning for you.
  Rotten grapes You are likely to experience a temporary financial setback.
  See also **Vineyards**

Grass If you are standing in fresh, green grass, you will enjoy good health and high energy levels, but if the grass is pale or dry, you could encounter a temporary setback in your health or financial affairs. If you are looking at fresh, green grass in the distance, your current stresses will be eased, although you may have to wait a short while.
  Cutting grass You may be finding your busy environment too crowded and stressful, and a change to a quieter, perhaps more

rural way of life could suit you better. However, if you are mowing a friend's grass, or someone asks you to do this for them, you may be better suited to an urban life since it is there that you will be able to prove yourself.

Grasshoppers This insect is an indication of good news and suggests a sudden change in your life for the better, possibly related to your happiness or spiritual development rather than your finances. This is especially true if you are holding it in your hand. You may also receive help from a friend.
A flight of grasshoppers This suggests a dramatic change, which will be chiefly for the better.
Killing a grasshopper This is a bad dream in that it suggests ill-health or a difficult period in your life.

Graves A grave symbolises justice, hope and good news. If you do not know the owner of the grave, take it as a symbol of hope if you are experiencing difficulties and a sign that you will receive justice in the end. If you are expecting an answer to a request, you may have to wait for the response but it will be a good one.
Your father's grave You will receive support.
Your mother's grave You will find encouragement for your plans.
Your child's grave This may be an emotional time for you and you are anxious to make changes in your life, perhaps to leave behind a period of negativity, or to become more settled.
Your brother's or sister's grave Face the challenges before you with honesty and a strong sense of purpose.
A friend's grave Make sure your dealings are honest and aboveboard if you want to achieve your objectives.
An enemy's grave You are calm and decided in your actions.
See also **Burial, Cemeteries, Funerals**

Graveyards *see* **Cemeteries**

Green *see* **Colours**

Grocers *see* **Shopkeepers**

Guns Any kind of gun in a dream symbolises uncertainty and an unreliable temper.

Holding a gun If you are holding the gun in your hand, you have a bad temper and are likely to fly off the handle without much provocation. If you are pointing the gun at someone, then your present difficulties are of your own making. If you are threatening your parents, then you are holding a grudge against society in general. If you are threatening your partner, you are over-stressed and nervous. If you are threatening your children, you are not taking their needs seriously.

Someone threatening you with a gun If the person is your partner, take steps to communicate with them and resolve any differences between you, as there is a chance that you cannot trust them and that they will be inclined to serve their own interests. If one of your parents is pointing a gun at you, think about whether your approach to life is sufficiently serious; only a considered way of life is likely to be successful.

See also **Weapons**

Gypsies A gypsy symbolises wandering, restlessness and instability. Seeing a group of gypsies in a dream, or talking with them, indicates a period of restlessness, when perhaps you will move or change your job. If you are aggressive towards a gypsy, then you are feeling unhappy with your present circumstances and feel the need to move on. If they promise you good luck in return for money, be cautious, as someone you are dealing with may not be totally honest. If you refuse to pay or ignore the requests, you will be successful.

Quarrelling with a gypsy You may encounter problems relating to a trip you have planned; see if you can postpone it for a week or two.

H

Hailstorms Hailstorms are usually associated with a sudden turn for the worse, most often concerned with business and social affairs.
A hailstorm over a city Your business deals could be under threat.
A hailstorm over countryside You could suffer some financial loss.
A hailstorm over a desert Changes will occur which are more likely to be for the better than for the worse.
A hailstorm over a stretch of water Be especially careful of your health as you could encounter problems in that area.
You are caught in a hailstorm This is indicative of a difficult period in your life when you may be led astray by those around you. Take care that you deal with honest people, both socially and in business or at work. If you have difficulty walking in the hailstorm, it is likely to be some time before you are able to extricate yourself from any current difficulties.

Hair If your own hair is grey or white and you dream that it has gone back to its original colour, you are feeling particularly energetic and have plenty of vitality; but if the reverse is true you need to take more care of your health. If your hair has turned golden or red, make sure you are dealing honestly with those around you and not behaving hypocritically. If your hair appears unusually long, you will overcome any recent difficulties.

Hairdressers Petty quarrels and hindrances in achieving your ambitions are symbolised by this dream. You may experience a period of financial difficulties.
Being a hairdresser This is an unfavourable dream, ultimately meaning that you will not mind indulging in immoral or illegal means to get what you want. It also means a general lowering of your standards.
Being with a hairdresser If they are outside the salon, this symbolises hypocrisy. If they are inside but not working, it means a tense period within the family as a result of misunderstandings.

Having your hair cut In this case, the dream indicates that you yourself are the cause of your own problems, although you may blame others. It also indicates a period of your life characterised by quarrels and general disappointments. If you ask the hairdresser to stop cutting your hair, it indicates that your problems are likely to be brief and you will achieve your ambitions despite a short setback.

Your hair is accidentally cut or shaved Misunderstandings that follow this dream will eventually be sorted out to everyone's satisfaction.

See also **Scissors**

Halos A halo symbolises spiritual gain or recovery from ill-health for the person on whom you see the halo.

A halo on your parents This indicates that they will enjoy a long and healthy life.

Someone tells you that you have a halo It is possible that you will be tricked in a business dealing and you will suffer loss as a result.

See also **Saints**

Hammers A hammer in a dream symbolises hard work, honesty and modest success.

Constructing something using a hammer You will have moderate financial success.

Hammering a nail into a door You are unwittingly blocking your own progress. Reconsider your actions and you may make better progress.

Breaking something with a hammer Uncertainty in business is likely.

Shaping an object with a hammer If you work hard, you will achieve your goals.

Threatening someone with a hammer Stress is likely to create problems for you. Find more time for relaxation.

Being threatened with a hammer If you know the person, look out for feelings of jealousy in those around you and deal with them in a sensitive way. If you do not recognise the person, be alert in case of a conspiracy surrounding you, even if it is only a minor one.

See also **Nails**

Hands Hands are a symbol of giving oneself a message.

Your right hand The right hand represents the things that are most important to you, especially your partner and children. If you see your right hand as clean and uninjured, you can look forward to a happy married life, or the prospect of marriage. If your spiritual life is more important to you than family, then you could look forward to spiritual gains. A dirty, deformed hand denotes disappointments and setbacks.

Your left hand Since your left hand represents your parents and siblings, a clean, healthy left hand indicates good relationships with them, while a dirty or misshapen one indicates arguments.

A child's hand Things are likely to change for the better in your life, possibly dramatically.

Hanging This is a favourable dream because death in any form suggests an end to one cycle but the beginning of another.

Being hanged If you see yourself being hanged in a dream but you are still alive, you still have a chance to replan your goals. If you have been hanged, you will have to continue with the ideals and goals you have already set and move ahead with care.

Seeing your father being hanged Whether he is actually alive or dead, this dream means that you will enjoy the same respect from others as he did.

Seeing your mother being hanged You will enjoy considerable respect from those around you.

See also **Death, Execution, Gallows**

Hats If you appear to be pleased that you are wearing a hat in your dream, you could look forward to some sudden financial gain, although if you are angry or upset, be more cautious or you could be the victim of fraud.

Buying a hat Problems and disappointments in your married life or among your close friends are indicated by this dream.

Holding a hat If your mood is positive in the dream, your hard work will be rewarded, but if you are angry or aggressive, then a business venture you are about to embark on may not turn out as successfully as you hoped.

Being given a hat You deserve the benefits you have worked for.

Snatching a hat from someone Don't make the mistake of taking actions that you know are wrong; you will not benefit.

Hay Dreaming of hay indicates the successful realisation of a project.
Hay spread around you You are on the right path to achieving your goals.
Hay in stacks Good news is on the horizon.
Hay on fire Stop depending on the advice of others too much and act more independently. If people are fighting the blaze, you will have trustworthy friends. If someone calls you to help fight the blaze, your efforts will soon come to fruition.

Heads A smiling and friendly head is a sign of good times to come, but an angry or unhappy head indicate misfortunes, usually caused by someone of the opposite sex. If the head is threatening, don't take unusual risks as they could make things worse.
A severed head If there is blood in the dream, it is organic (see page 9) and has no significance, but if not, it is an indication of bad news in the family, perhaps serious.
Your own head If your head is normal, you will receive a reward of some kind. If it is severed, beware of hypocrites.

Hearses A hearse symbolises a sudden change in your life. If it is moving towards your house, it is a sign of unexpected gains. If you happen to see one pass by, expect a good period with plenty of support from your friends. If the hearse is carrying a member of your family or a close friend, you can expect a new beginning for the family.
See also **Coffins, Funerals**

Hell If you dream of hell, you are likely to be at a turning point in your life where things could be changed for the better.
Being in hell Muster your strongest determination to begin a more meaningful life.
Burning in hell You are likely to be feeling stressed by pangs of conscience because of some of your former behaviour.
Escaping from hell This is a good sign that you will improve your current situation.
Seeing friends in hell You will have to face problems in the future because of what is going on around you at the moment. Be more aware of the behaviour of others towards you.
See also **Devils**

Herbs An auspicious dream which can be interpreted in various ways depending on your current circumstances. It could mean better health, resolution of arguments or financial gain.
Herbs growing all around you You can look forward to great happiness.
Herbs tied in bundles You should enjoy continued good health or recovery if you have been ill. If you have been unemployed, your job prospects will improve over the next few months.
Being offered herbs If the herbs are fresh, this indicates good news or the end to a family argument. If you eat the herbs you are given, this indicates that you have a strong interest in education or science.
Buying herbs You are showing a determination to solve your problems.
Selling herbs You are more likely to be able to offer your help to those around you than to receive it from them.

Hills A range of hills indicates a challenge in life and this is a dream only usually experienced by those with a strong sense of ambition. Seeing a single hill indicates that you will have barriers to cross; the more hills you see, the more barriers you will come up against or the more testing they will be. However, you are likely to overcome obstacles and be pleased with your achievements.
Standing on top of a hill Your future will be profitable as you have always been honest in your dealings with people.

Hockey Playing hockey on ice or grass denotes a desire to enter business which is likely to come about.

Honey Honey symbolises good health, modesty, hard work and truth.
Honey in a comb You are straightforward and hard-working; if you take honey from a comb, you are likely to realise your modest goals very quickly.
Honey in jars or bottles You will have a steady but contented way of life.
Eating honey You want to retain your independence, but if you are eating with other people, then you can enter into a joint business venture without jeopardising that and with some success.

Offering honey to others to eat You are shy and retiring in your personality.

Being offered honey to eat You will have more than one option to consider when you are thinking about achieving your modest ambitions.

See also **Bees**

Horns Animal horns, being natural, symbolise good luck and prosperity. Horns on people, on the other hand, indicate fraud, evil intentions and hypocrisy. If you see a lot of horns hanging on a wall or lying around, it means that you should be careful of too much extravagance.

A cow's horn There is likely to be an expansion in your business or promotion or improvement of some kind at work.

A goat's horn This signifies wealth through inheritance or an expensive gift.

A sheep's horn Good news is on the way.

You grow horns However large or small they are, seeing yourself with horns in a dream indicates that you have been or are being dishonest in some way, either towards yourself or others.

Someone tells you that you have horns If you cannot see the horns, the dream is a direct warning that you should change your course of action or it will create problems for you, perhaps even legal ones.

Someone else has horns If you recognise them, that person is likely to make some wrong decision which could land them in trouble. If they are a stranger, be careful not to trust new acquaintances until you know them better.

Horses A horse in a dream generally indicates promotion and stability.

Feeding a horse You will enjoy continued good health or recovery from illness.

Grooming or petting a horse You are fortunate in that you have trustworthy friends.

Riding a horse You will be offered good work opportunities.

A horse galloping away There may be a break in your marriage or personal relationships.

See also **Riding, Saddles, Stables**

Hospitals Dreaming of a hospital usually indicates recovery from ill-health or depression. If you are actually ill, you will make at least a partial recovery quite soon.
Leaving a hospital A calm period in your life is indicated.
A make-shift or field hospital This is not an auspicious dream as it can indicate an accident or a natural disaster affecting you in some way.
See also **Doctors, Illness, Nurses**

Hounds If you see hounds in a hunt, it means hard work will be needed to achieve your goals.
A hound near you You will enjoy political success.
Feeding hounds You have strong spiritual values.
See also **Dogs, Hunting**

Houses A house in a dream symbolises improvement in living standards if it is your own house. If it is a former house, it may indicate that you regret moving away. If you have never owned a house and you dream of one, it could indicate that you will have the chance to have a house of your own one day.
Being in a house with your family A period of calm will follow a time of stress and instability and you will be tolerant and understanding towards your family.
Speaking with your family about buying a house You are likely to be involved in the purchase of property within a year.
See also **Buying**

Humiliation This is a dream of contrary meaning, indicating success and respect. If someone is jealous or resentful of you, they will come to recognise your worth.
Humiliating others Your pride and ego are too strong but you will learn to respect other people.

Hunchbacks This dream indicates good news or a modest but enjoyable life, as long as you do not quarrel with the hunchback.
A hunchback speaks to you in a friendly way You will have a positive response to a question.
A hunchback hugs you You will have a long period of happiness.
Arguing with a hunchback Your difficulties will be of your own making.

A hunchback gives you bad news You can expect a time of arguments with partner or friends.

Hunger If you are poor and dream of being hungry, the next few days are likely to be full of surprises and you will receive help from outside. However, if you are comfortably off and dream of being hungry, you are still not content with what you have. If you are in business, there are some impending problems demanding resolution. If they are not resolved, you will suffer considerable cost.
Your children are hungry If you are helpless to do anything for your hungry children, you will not be forgotten by your friends when you need their support.
See also **Famine, Starvation**

Hunting If you are invited to attend a hunt in your dream, you will receive good news that will radically change your life.
Hunting birds You have a tendency to be undependable.
Hunting dangerous animals, such as tigers or bears You have the courage and wisdom to overcome challenges.
Hunting a pregnant animal You have a cruel or immoral streak in your nature that you would do well to curb.
Hunting rabbits or similar animals Your constructive approach is the right one to succeed.
See also **Hounds**

Husbands If you and your husband or partner appear to be getting on well in the dream, then this is likely to happen in life as well, probably as a result of your own sensitivity. If he is angry and shouting at you, there is a misunderstanding between you which you need to work to resolve. If you have been honest with him, it will work out. If you have something to hide, he may leave you to be happier elsewhere.

Hyenas Seeing a hyena in the distance can be seen as a warning to disassociate yourself from certain colleagues or acquaintances before they bring you trouble.
Hyenas feeding on a dead animal You should be very wary of being overtrusting in your work or business affairs.
A pack of hyenas You are worried about something, but if you frighten them away, you will also overcome difficulties.

Feeding a hyena This dream underlines your tendency towards greed.

Hymns Hymns in a dream symbolise compassion for others, a strong social conscience and a life of virtue.

Singing hymns You have a selfless character. If you are singing with others, you will go a long way towards helping those less fortunate than yourself, while those around you are also compassionate and likely to work for charity. If the group includes your partner and children, you will have a happy married life.

I

Ice Ice in a dream denotes financial loss, misunderstandings and arguments. It can also indicate illness. Vast expanses of ice indicate business losses and continued risks if you carry on in the same profession.
Standing on an icy expanse Be careful of your health as you may suffer illness soon, although you should soon recover.
Floating ice Seeing large chunks of ice floating on a stretch of water signifies a temporary setback in life as a result of your unrealistic attitude. If disputes between you and your partner continue, they could end in separation. Small pieces of ice floating on a pond or pool indicate petty squabbles which will eventually be resolved.

Idols These are an indication of false hopes and unrealistic expectations. They can also reflect a strong materialistic nature. It could be that you want to achieve your ambitions without any effort on your part, or that you could try underhand means to get what you want. If the idols are made of stone, you are inclined to be petty and fraudulent. If they are of gold or silver, take care that you do not associate with cheats.
Praying in front of an idol Your motivation is fame and fortune and you will go to almost any lengths to achieve it.
Breaking an idol Although you may have acted in a fraudulent way, you know what you should do and will find the strength to do it.

Illness This is very much a dream of opposites. If you are really ill and you dream of illness, you will recover. If you are not ill, the dream suggests continued good health.
Someone else being ill The outcome will be good for them.
Your parents are ill They will live a long and healthy life.
Your partner or child is ill You will be happily married.
Your friend is ill Your friendship will grow.
Someone you have argued with is ill You will be reconciled.
See also **Doctors, Hospitals, Nurses, Pain, Recovering from illness**

Infidelity Another dream that indicates the opposite of what you see. If you are behaving unfaithfully in the dream, it underlines that you are honest and faithful in life, both to your partner and friends. If someone else in the dream is being unfaithful to you, they have great love and admiration for you.

Ingots A gold ingot indicates important developments for anyone in business or the possibility of employment for those who are unemployed. It also shows a pregnant woman that she will have a healthy child and tells a sick person that they will recover. An ingot made of another metal, however, is not as auspicious as it can indicate that what looks good may not turn out to be so.
Holding an ingot Holding a gold ingot means that time is on your side, while a silver one symbolises good business partners.
Buying an ingot If you buy a gold ingot, you have a tendency towards greed which should be checked, but if you buy a silver ingot, you are less ambitious and more contented.
Stealing an ingot You are unsure of your own plans in life but greed will not solve them for you.

Ink Depending on the circumstances in the dream, ink can indicate good and bad outcomes.
Ink in a bottle This is a good dream symbolising that you will shortly embark on a new plan or a new period in your life.
Ink stains Ink stains on your body indicate hardships and setbacks, while on your hands they indicate financial loss or poor health. If you see ink stains on your face, someone may be trying to tarnish your reputation.
Spilt ink Ink spilt on the ground or on paper denotes good news or a present from a member of the family or from someone close to you.
Buying ink This indicates that you have a determination to succeed and, while you may have to wait, you will have success.

Innocence To dream that you have been found innocent of something or have been acquitted of something signifies better times for you in the future. It also indicates that people have misjudged you.
Being found innocent by your friends Such a dream means that you will enter into a new period of life full of calm and tranquillity and will earn the respect and confidence of others.

Being found innocent of wrongdoing by the law Such a dream suggests that there has been a period of misunderstanding between you and your family but that they will eventually come to understand and respect you.

Finding others innocent or forgiving them If you forgive or acquit others for any misunderstanding or problem, this dream indicates that, without realising it, you are acquiring spiritual strength.

See also **Courts of law, Judges**

Insanity Dreaming that you are mad is not necessarily a bad dream. If you are married or about to marry, it indicates that you will enjoy a happy married life with mutual respect between you. However, if you show signs of insanity in front of someone else, then you are likely to argue with them, whether it is your partner, employer, friends or children.

Other people appear insane This dream does not have good indications. If it is your partner, it could mean serious misunderstandings between you, and if it is any member of your family, it could indicate arguments. If it is your parents, you may not have applied yourself too seriously in life. If it is your siblings, you are too conceited. If your friends appear insane, their friendships could be superficial.

Insults Insulting and being insulted in a dream both indicate a weakness of character or emotional disturbances.

Insulting someone If you recognise the person, make sure you are not taking revenge for some past action. If you do not recognise them, you are likely to be under emotional pressure and should try to find ways to relieve the stress. If you insult an elderly person, it denotes that you lack confidence in yourself. If you insult someone of the same sex, you could be jealous of someone close to you. If you insult someone of the opposite sex, you are not serious in your attitude to relationships.

Being insulted If you are insulted by your father or mother, it is an indication that you should be more realistic in life. If you are insulted by your partner, make sure your behaviour is not reckless. If you are insulted by friends, think about whether you have been absolutely honest with them lately.

See also **Arguments, Humiliation**

Interviews

Being interviewed If you are being interviewed by an employer, you attach a great deal of importance to your job. If you are being interviewed by a writer, it reflects a desire to have more prominence or a public position. If a teacher is interviewing you, you may be worrying about an evaluation test at work, or an exam or test of some kind. You are showing that you have doubts about yourself if you see yourself being interviewed by a judge or court official, and if the person is a police officer, you could encounter legal problems. If a doctor is interviewing you about your health, you could suffer minor health problems.

Interviewing others If they are of the opposite sex, it indicates domestic worries. If they are of the same sex, it can indicate that you are jealous of someone.

Islands An island in a dream symbolises your desire to achieve something single-handedly. However, depending on the circumstances, it can also indicate a sense of loneliness or isolation. If you see a green island in the distance, you may experience delays in achieving what you set out to do. If the island is barren, you need to make more effort. The nearer the island, the closer the realisation of your dreams.

Being on an island If the island is inhabited, you can count on the support of friends and family. If the island is deserted, look to the realism of your plans and perhaps redirect them in a more constructive way.

Ivory Ivory can denote prosperity and riches at the cost of others, or happiness and good health, depending on the circumstances.

Tusks on a live elephant This signifies that your wealth is growing and healthy. If you touch the tusks of the elephant, you will have great prosperity, happiness and good health.

Ivory goods in a shop or wearing ivory This indicates that you are living at the expense of others. If you see someone else wearing ivory, the dream foretells a long term of unemployment, loss or even problems with the law.

Buying or selling ivory If you buy ivory, you are surrounded by unscrupulous people who may try to ruin you. If you sell ivory, you should be careful that you are not living immorally, although if you discard the ivory, you may have the will-power to change and lead a virtuous life.

See also **Elephants**

J

Jackets A jacket symbolises protection from danger or, in some circumstances, success at work.

Wearing or holding a jacket You will soon reach a stage in your life and your career when you will be able to support both yourself and your family, and also help those less fortunate than you. If the jacket is old, you are likely to remain in the same line of business.

A jacket in a shop This dream indicates protection from a business or financial loss through the intervention of friends.

Buying or selling a jacket This indicates that you want to have an independent profession.

Jade Jade is a symbol of vitality, happiness and prosperity. It also indicates a return to good health for those who have been ill, or a recovery from stress or emotional difficulties, or even from financial setbacks.

Holding a piece of jade Such a dream means that luck is with you. Though it will not necessarily bring you riches, it will certainly bring you happiness and contentment.

Jam Jam in a dream symbolises sudden and fairly drastic changes in your life, not necessarily for the better. The lighter the colour of the jam, the more positive the change is likely to be, so that a pale jam suggests that you should look for a change to your present circumstances, whereas a dark-coloured jam indicates a sudden change which may be difficult to accept.

Buying jam Buying jam indicates boredom with your life. Perhaps you should instigate some changes.

Selling jam You are not comfortable with your present companions and want to find a better milieu.

Making jam This indicates that you are searching for calm and happiness and are not yet sure where you will find it.

Eating jam This indicates your attitude to life in general. The darker the colour, the more emotional your reactions; the lighter the colour, the more you allow reason to guide you.

Jesus Christ Seeing a figure of Jesus Christ in a dream has several wonderful interpretations and it is rarely dreamed by anyone with a vicious nature. If you are a priest or minister, this dream indicates your deep attachment to spiritual values. If you are ill, your recovery is indicated. If you are living a normal life, you will find your spiritual values deepened and enriched by this dream, and if you have things in your past which you regret, you will be able to live a better life in future.

Jesus Christ speaks to you You are on the right path in life and you should continue in the same way. If you have experienced difficulties or emotional trauma, you will find the strength to move beyond them.

Jewellery Jewellery in a dream symbolises success, health and happiness. It can also indicate true friendship. If you are in business, it indicates further success and, if not, the beginnings of a better future. If you are ill, you are likely to get better. If you have argued with your partner, family or friends, you should be able to find reconciliation.

Receiving a gift of jewellery If your father gives you jewellery, it indicates his continued affection and support. If your partner gives you jewellery, it shows they are faithful and loving. A gift of jewellery from your employer could presage a promotion.

Finding jewellery Your successes will be due to your own endeavours.

See also **Diamonds, Earrings, Ingots, Pearls, Rings, Silver**

Judges If you meet and talk amicably with a judge, your life will continue to go well and you may even expect success at work.

Appearing before a judge in court If the judge looks or acts with severity, you should take the dream as a warning that something you have done in the recent past was illegal or at least immoral. If you are forgiven, you will be able to rectify the situation.

Being a judge This reflects various potential talents within you. Utilise them and you will find happiness and even perhaps financial gain.

See also **Courts of law, Innocence, Lawyers**

Jugglers A juggler in a dream symbolises artificial happiness, indecision and potential failure. Especially if you recognise the juggler, take it as a warning that you depend too much on false hopes and unrealistic ways of thinking.

Being a juggler You are being unrealistic, at best, in your work environment and things will not work out as you would like them to. Make changes quickly to avoid problems.

Jumping The nature of the obstacle and the success of your actions in the dream indicate different possibilities.

Jumping over something If you successfully jump over a small obstacle such as a hole, a rock or a log, then your success at work is likely to be short-lived as you are not making enough effort to maximise your talents. If you stumble while jumping, your perseverance and objective approach will enable you to succeed.

Jumping from a considerable height Be more careful where financial matters are concerned.

Seeing others jumping An auspicious dream indicating a success requiring a celebration. If anyone falls over while jumping, your friends will be there to help you when you need them.

Jungles Seeing a dense jungle in a dream symbolises unexpected problems, due either to your own negligence or to unscrupulous business partners. The closer the jungle, the closer the problem. The denser the jungle, the more complex the problem.

Being in a jungle If you appear frightened, it means you are uncertain as to your future actions. If you appear lost, it means some past activity will bear negative results. You should refrain from getting involved in any new business venture.

Finding a way out of a jungle Determined efforts on your part will finally help you to overcome any present difficulties.

K

Keels The keel of a ship or boat, whether metal, wooden or fibreglass, usually indicates the end of an unhappy period and the beginning of a new phase. If the keel is well crafted, that new phase will be a good one for you.
An upturned or damaged keel This is not such an auspicious dream. It denotes that you have been weak in facing the realities of life. An upturned keel in the water indicates that you have been unrealistic and extravagant.

Kettles Dreaming about kettles has a variety of interpretations, usually to do with overcoming problems of some kind.
An empty kettle You feel uncertain about your plans and aspirations.
A full kettle You are likely to be involved in petty arguments which could spiral out of control. If the kettle is being boiled, you will find the courage to deal with any problems that occur.
A burnt-out, misshapen or unusable kettle This dream means an end to stress.
Being given a shiny, new kettle You will begin a new life that will compensate for your past.
Throwing a kettle You will have difficulty overcoming your problems.

Keys Dreaming about keys indicates the realisation of modest aspirations. This may be concerned with the fields of marriage, partnerships, education or work.
A large, old key You are likely to receive money through an inheritance.
Holding several keys You are likely to have to make a choice between various opportunities.
Being given a key You are likely to be given some unexpected help so that you can start a new phase in your life.
Finding a key You will solve your own problems.
Losing a key You are in a period of emotional stress and may need support and help from others to overcome your difficulties.
See also **Locks**

Kidnapping Not a favourable dream, this has a number of different interpretations depending on the circumstances.

Witnessing a kidnap Your plans will not work out well. If you recognise any of the criminals, you should disassociate yourself from anyone whose honesty you doubt.

Someone asks you to help in a kidnap If you agree to help, you are likely to experience a difficult period marked by arguments and financial difficulties. If you refuse, things will soon get better.

You assist in a kidnap Your future has a bleak outlook unless you raise your moral standards.

You are kidnapped You are attaching too much confidence to your own abilities.

Killing There are various interpretations of killing or being killed in a dream.

Killing your father or mother You are ungrateful or wicked.

Killing your brother or sister You have a jealous nature.

Killing your partner Exercise calm and restraint otherwise an argument with your partner will have serious consequences.

Killing a beggar or homeless person You have turned away from spiritual values.

Killing a friend You will have a lonely and sad life for some time to come.

Killing a priest or clergyman You need to make drastic changes in your life if it is not to continue on a downhill path.

Killing a police officer or other person associated with the law There is potential for legal problems if you continue to act in the same way.

Being asked to kill someone If you accept, you will continue on a negative path. If you refuse, you value your future and have the potential to make things better.

Asking someone else to kill a person You still harbour a grudge against a member of your family.

Someone kills you You are not taking proper care of your health and you may suffer a short illness. If you recognise the person as your partner or a friend, it denotes that your uncompromising nature could lead you into difficulties.

See also **Assassins**

Kings The interpretation of this dream will vary according to the mood of the king. If the king in your dream is friendly and relaxed, you are likely to be helped by your parents. An angry king indicates impending arguments in the home and a sad king denotes a difficult period for you.

A king sitting down If the king is sitting with others, it indicates that any accusations levelled against you will prove false, while if he is sitting alone, you will recover from any stress or depression you experience in the near future. If he is sitting on a throne, it symbolises success.

A king visits you or sends you an invitation This is a sure sign of success for you.

A dead king Your sadness and problems will be dispelled sooner or later.

Being a king This is a dream of contrary meaning which forebodes unemployment and financial setbacks. If you are prosperous in real life, your financial status will go down.

Giving or taking something from a king This dream is an exceptionally good sign of sudden financial advantages or honour through your own effects.

See also **Palaces, Queens**

Kissing Happiness and an end to misunderstandings are indicated by a kiss in a dream. It also symbolises friendship.

Being kissed If your father kisses you, he is pleased with you. If you are ill in real life and your father kisses you, you will soon recover. If your mother kisses you, you are leading a normal life and if your siblings kiss you, they value your support. If your partner kisses you, it is a mark of your mutual respect. If any of your friends kiss you, it is a sign of their friendship.

Kissing others Kissing your friends, business partners or colleagues indicates success while kissing any of your siblings means an end to your worries. Kissing your parents indicates your grateful character. Kissing the hands of a king, a clergyman or any holy person indicates that you will achieve your modest goals in life.

Kitchens If the kitchen is large and clean with food on the table, it indicates a happy and harmonious home. An untidy kitchen means differences of opinion will arise in the family.

Food being cooked in the kitchen This denotes a visit from a friend or the satisfactory results of your efforts.

People eating in the kitchen If your family are eating, this is a sign of good health. If friends are eating there, it is a sign of financial prosperity or a reason for a small celebration. If you see yourself eating alone, you want to remain independent but there is also a danger of isolation. If you are eating with friends, a good project will soon be proposed to you.

See also **Cooking, Eating**

Kites A kite symbolises ambitions, perhaps beset with difficulties. If the kite is flying high, your ambitions may be too big to be realistic. If it is flying low, your plans may be more modest, but they are more likely to succeed.

A kite diving towards the ground A temporary halt to a business venture might be advisable.

Flying a kite If you find it easy to control the kite, you will not find too many difficulties ahead of you, but if you find difficulty controlling the kite, you are likely to experience an unsteady life dotted with setbacks.

A kite becoming entangled Difficulties could be ahead of you, which may be of a legal nature.

Knights Courage, kindness, truth and help for the less fortunate are all indicated by a knight in a dream. A knight in armour or on horseback indicates that you possess the courage within you to fight any injustice you encounter. If the knight greets you or speaks in a friendly way, any arguments with friends will be resolved and any accusations against you will prove to be false. Several knights denote trustworthy friends.

Being a knight A good dream, reflecting your kindness. If you dream of fighting an enemy, it symbolises your strong love for truth and your helpful nature.

Knives A knife symbolises illness, arguments, loss of money and setbacks. A small knife is a reminder to control your emotions, while a large knife indicates family quarrels or arguments with friends. A rusty knife indicates the end of tensions and setbacks.

Using a cooking knife in a kitchen You have a cautious approach to life.

Threatening someone with a knife If you threaten someone else with a knife, you are likely to suffer from a minor illness.
Being threatened with a knife This can mean financial loss which may be serious.
Buying a knife Controlling your temper will be to your advantage.
See also **Cuts, Daggers, Sharpening, Wounds**

Knots If you dream of a single knot on a string, it denotes an impending setback, perhaps financial. It can also mean quarrels with your friends. On a rope, it signifies a more significant business or financial failure. Several smaller knots on a string symbolise a number of small obstacles that you will encounter, while if they are on a rope, they are likely to be of a more serious nature.
Tying a knot You have been careless and this could cause you problems in the future if you do not rectify the situation.
Undoing a knot You will quickly disentangle yourself from your present problems.
See also **Ropes**

L

Labourers Ability, talent, honesty and a contented life are
indicated by dreaming of a labourer or factory worker.
A metal worker indicates good health and a farm worker
denotes a productive life.
Being a labourer If you appear as a labourer in your dream and
you are not one in real life, you will always be contented with
what you have.
See also **Bricklayers, Carpenters**

Ladders A ladder symbolises gains and profits, success in your
projects and achieving your dreams. If the ladder is against a
wall, a little effort on your part will be all that is required. If the
ladder is lying on the ground, you will have to work harder but
success will be yours.
Climbing a ladder You will achieve the success you have been
working for. If you are at the top of the ladder, you may be
unaware of the success you have been having. If you have
difficulty climbing the ladder or fall off halfway up, you may
experience setbacks but they will only be temporary.
See also **Climbing**

Lakes A huge lake of clear and calm water suggests the end of a
long and difficult period for you. If the water is rough or dirty,
you will continue to experience difficulties for some time, but
they will come to an end.
Swimming in a lake You have taken good care of yourself and
you will remain in good health.
See also **Swimming, Water**

Lameness Seeing a lame person in a dream indicates difficulties. If
you do not recognise the individual, you are spending too much
money and time on useless projects. If you do recognise the lame
person, one of your family may experience some ill-health.
Being lame This is a good omen, suggesting that you will never
be disgraced in life.

Lamps A lamp in a dream symbolises beneficial guidance and, if it is
shining brightly, success through truth and personal ability.

Someone holding a lamp A friend will help and support you. If you are holding the lamp, you will succeed through your own efforts.

Lighting a lamp You are laying the foundations of a new phase of your life.

Landscapes The landscape in which you find yourself can be taken as an indication of your attitude to life in general. A beautiful landscape with lush, green fields foretells a happy period, while a barren or rocky one signifies a difficult time ahead for you with potential losses if you are not very cautious.

See also **Countryside**

Laughter Seeing yourself laughing in a dream is likely to mean that a time of unhappiness, difficulties and trials may lie ahead. It may involve the ill-health of a family member.

Other people laughing Your problems will abate somewhat. If the people are your family or close friends, things will get better much more quickly.

Lawsuits This is generally a dream with a positive interpretation, depending on who is filing the suit against you. If it is your partner, you will enjoy a good relationship. If it is an old woman, it indicates that you will not suffer any legal problems. If it is an old man, however, someone close to you may not have your true interests at heart.

Someone tells you a suit has been filed against you If you do not know the name of the person, any attempts to discredit you will not be successful. If you tell someone you intend to file a lawsuit, beware of stress levels in your daily life as you have become too nervous.

Lawyers A lawyer in a dream symbolises misunderstandings, fraud, jealousy or conspiracies. If the lawyer is an acquaintance and you appear to be engaging in friendly conversation with him or her, family problems are indicated. If the lawyer is unfriendly or angry, it is a sign that there is something fraudulent in your past which you would do well to deal with. If the lawyer is offering you advice, watch out for conspiracies or jealousy surrounding you.

Being defended by a lawyer Mistakes you have made in the past will catch up with you and cause you problems. If you ask a lawyer to defend your case and they accept, it is possible that you have been the victim of an injustice, while if they refuse, you will win any lawsuits or arguments you are involved with in the near future.

Being a lawyer You will defend yourself against difficult odds.

See also **Courts of law, Judges, Lawsuits**

Leaders The significance of this dream is very much determined by the personality of the leader. If the individual is a despot, it indicates unhappy developments to come, but if they are or were popular, it suggests promotion at work and success in business.

Being a leader Your life is becoming too stressful and this dream is a reflection of your nervous state. Try to find time to relax and ways to view life more calmly.

A leader with a threatening weapon You are likely to have a particularly difficult period ahead.

A wicked leader dead This signifies calm after a long and stormy period.

Leaves Leaves in a dream symbolise good health and prosperity.

Green leaves on a tree This is a good sign indicating continued good health and success at work. For lovers, it signifies mutual understanding.

Dried leaves If you dream of dried leaves on a tree or on the ground, this indicates a possible argument with your partner.

Touching leaves Touching green leaves on a tree indicates that you will have a love affair, while touching dried leaves can be taken as a sign of poor health.

See also **Trees**

Lemons Lemons symbolise a bitter period, involving family misunderstandings and even arguments with your partner, especially if the lemons are growing on the tree. Dreaming about a basket of lemons makes the problems more severe.

Buying lemons This dream indicates a sense of restlessness within you. Perhaps it is time to make some changes in your life.

Cutting lemons Cutting or squeezing lemons reflects a sense of anger and frustration.

Eating lemons A bitter period is in store for you, marked particularly by arguments with those closest to you. You may also experience a down-turn in your health.

Lepers Lepers in a dream symbolise guilt and animosity. If they simply pass you by, it is a sign of a temporary financial setback.
A leper threatens you You have enemies masquerading as friends.
A leper speaks with you This indicates an impending quarrel with your partner.
Being a leper This dream is a sign of the guilt you are carrying for the way you have been behaving. You have caused problems for others and are suffering as a result. If you are suddenly cured, it is a sign that you will find a way to make amends for your past behaviour and will act in a more caring way in future.

Letters Writing letters symbolises good news, hope and support. If you do not know who you are writing to, it simply means that you can expect good news.
A letter to a doctor You are likely to recover quickly from any health problems.
A letter to a friend You have every confidence in them.
A letter to your parents You have a strong love for them.
Receiving a letter Receiving letters in a dream is generally a sign of support. If the letter is from your parents, it suggests that good news is on the way, while if the letter is from your siblings, you will find the support you need when it is most required. A letter concerning employment suggests you will need to be patient.

Libraries A library is a symbol of a realistic approach to life and if you see a library from outside, it confirms that you are a straightforward and law-abiding person.
Being inside a library You are trying to find reasons for problems you have had of late. If someone suggests a book you should read, then you can expect advice from someone which will be helpful.
You are invited into a library You will have the support you need over the coming weeks.
Sleeping in a library You are wasting time.
See also **Books**

Life-saving Saving a life or being saved is a suggestion that you will have a good life and be protected from harm.

Being saved If you are saved from drowning, luck will help you out of your present difficulties. If you are saved from falling, your family will help you out of a tough spot. If you are saved from being run over, your own skills will be the remedy for your problems. If you are saved from a murder attempt, it suggests a recovery. If your father saves you from anything, it suggests a safe life. If you are saved from injustice, it suggests justice will be on your side.

Saving someone This dream suggests that you can achieve your ambitions sooner or later. If the person is elderly or one of your parents, then this is an especially auspicious dream. Saving an animal is also a sign of a good life devoid of any major problems.
See also **Drowning**

Lighthouses Guidance, success and a safe journey are all indicated by dreaming of a lighthouse. If you are in a boat when you see the lighthouse, you will soon have a safe and fruitful journey, and if you already have a business trip planned, it will certainly be a success. If the light is bright, then your plans are sound, but if the light is dim, perhaps you should take another look at your intentions as it may be that they can be improved.

Lightning Lightning in a dream is a sign that a difficult period is coming to an end, and the significance will relate to your current needs in your waking state. It may mean that your health will improve, or that your employment prospects will take a turn for the better, or that you will make a good profit in business. However, if you are contemplating something unkind or even illegal, it could be taken as a warning that it will not turn out for the best.

Lightning striking a tree or a structure Especially if you are creative, this is a sign that you will be appreciated and highly regarded.

Lilies Lilies in dreams are symbols of honesty and affection.
Lilies in a field This dream emphasises your honest behaviour.
Being offered lilies You are likely to receive affection from those around you.
Offering lilies to someone You have high moral standards.

Lions A lion in a dream generally relates to perseverance, compassion and hard work.

A friendly lion You are likely to be comfortably well off.

Touching a lion You have a compassionate nature. If the lion roars at you when you touch it, reconsider your plans.

A roaring lion You are likely to receive a sudden promotion at work or achieve a business success.

A lion threatening you You have a tendency to be authoritarian.

A lioness Seeing a lioness in a dream indicates encouragement.

Lips Lips in a dream relate to your immediate situation in life. If they are normal and friendly, you are handling your affairs in a sensible way. The state of your own lips in a dream is indicative of the state of your health.

Bleeding lips You may have a quarrel with a distant family member.

Unfriendly, sealed lips You should make some changes in your life or face the consequences. If you take action, you will improve your circumstances.

Wide-apart lips You are about to encounter some problems.

See also **Mouths**

Lizards Hypocrisy and enmity are indicated by a lizard in a dream. If there is more than one lizard, it indicates that a close relative or friend is not as friendly as they seem and an increase of animosity between you is likely.

A lizard quite near you You have a carelessness towards life.

Killing a lizard You have a desire to begin a new phase in your life.

A dead lizard Any conspiracies against you will be futile.

Loan companies Seeing a premises relating to borrowing or lending money indicates that you are likely to have several creditors. If you enter the premises, it indicates financial loss due to carelessness.

Locks A lock can indicate either safety or an obstruction.

A new lock You will have good protection from harm.

A rusty and inoperable lock Someone is trying to block your efforts but they will not be successful.

Trying to open a lock You are likely to find some obstacles in your path. If the lock opens easily, you will overcome them without much difficulty. If you find it difficult to open the lock, you will have similar difficulties in your life, although you are likely to be successful in the end.
See also **Keys**

Locomotives *see* **Trains**

Love If you dream you are falling in love, it is often a sign that you are lonely in real life and are seeking companionship. If you know the person you fall in love with, the chances are that you will never speak with them. If you do not know them, you are likely to meet someone and form a relationship but it will not necessarily be long-lasting. If, in your dream, you fall in love with a former friend, consider whether you still have deep feelings for them.

Luggage Breakdowns, separation and homelessness can all be indicated by luggage in a dream so it is a warning to be particularly careful and sensitive in your relationships with others.
Someone carrying away luggage There is a strong possibility that you will argue with them, especially if it is your partner.
Going away with your luggage A period of homelessness or restlessness lies ahead of you.
See also **Bags**

M

Madness *see* **Insanity**

Mansions Dreams of mansions, palaces or castles indicate grandeur, power and continuity. They also symbolise long life and good health. However, they do not necessarily foretell considerable wealth or prosperity. The more imposing the property, the greater the significance of the dream. If you see a mansion in your dreams, your financial situation is likely to improve and the confidence you have will inspire greater respect in others. You may be in line for a official appointment. The significance increases if the building is close to you.
Being in a mansion You will soon be holding a responsible social or political position, but you must take a serious attitude towards achieving your goals.
See also **Palaces**

Marble If you see a large piece of uncut marble, it indicates prosperity as long as you follow a cautious and logical approach. If you see blocks of cut marble, you may be too extravagant in your lifestyle. If there are cracks in the marble, you will suffer business losses. If you pick up a piece of marble, you will endeavour to overcome problems in your life which are of your own making.
Buying marble You should experience an end to any financial problems.
Selling marble This can be an indication of family disputes.

Markets A market place symbolises plenty, good health and generally a good life, whether you see it from a distance or from close by. If it is crowded with people, you are likely to have considerable spending power. If you are in the market with friends or family, that is a good sign relating to sound family relationships. However, if you are alone, it can denote an egotistical streak which you would do well to curb. If you are completely alone, with no one else in the market, that egotism is leading you to take too many risks and they will not always pay off.

Marriage If you are unmarried and dream of marrying someone who does not return your affection, you are never likely to have a relationship with them, and that will be to your benefit.
Watching a wedding This could be a reflection of your own personal unhappiness. If you are married and dream of your own wedding, it could be an indication that you are not altogether happy in your relationship. Try to work harder at it and endeavour to avoid any potential problems.
A commotion at a wedding ceremony This indicates that arguments are on the cards, with either your partner or friends.
See also **Polygamy, Proposals of marriage, Remarriage**

Masks A mask is a symbol of fraud, cheating and slyness. If the mask is not being worn, you have a chance to change some of your behaviour before the consequences become negative. The more masks you see, the more serious the situation.
Someone wearing a mask Whether it is you or someone else, it is a sign that that person is not honest and you should be careful of your relationships with them.

Meat Large pieces of meat are a sign of a favourable financial deal, while small pieces indicate a modest gain.
Cooked meat You should enjoy continuing good health.
Meat thrown on the ground A short illness is likely.
Eating meat If you are eating a normal portion, that is a good general sign, but if you are being excessively greedy, then it indicates that you are overstressed and this is likely to lead you into disagreements with others.
Buying or selling meat Either of these circumstances in a dream indicates that you trust those around you.
See also **Butchers**

Medals Truth, respect, success and honour are indicated by dreaming of medals.
Wearing medals There are good times ahead of you, marked by the respect of others. If you are running for office of some kind, it is a particular indication of your courage and honesty and the respect other people have for you.
Someone else is wearing medals If you know the person, this underlines your truth and honesty. If you do not know them, it means you will have thoughtful and dependable friends.

Medicine This symbolises ill–health and unhappiness so you should take it as a warning to be particularly careful of your health. If there are several bottles of medicine in the dream, the illness could be serious and could affect a member of your family.
See also **Pharmacies**

Men If you see a well-dressed and well-presented man in your dreams, you will have a normal life. If the man is particularly, although not unnaturally, tall, your ambitions may be too high. If you see a man you know but who appears very small in the dream, this is a sign that you could be underestimating your own potential.
A naked man If it is someone you know, it is an indication of prosperity.
A dead man This indicates a long and healthy life for you.

Milk Milk in a container signifies joy, but spilt milk indicates indecisiveness.
Buying milk You have a wish to seek for the good and honest things in life.
Drinking milk This indicates that you are either in good health or will shortly return to good health.
Selling milk You have a clear vision of an honest life.
Throwing milk away You are undecided about your next move and need to concentrate to think through the issues at stake in order to make the right decision.

Mines Seeing a functioning mine with workers in your dream indicates that you must take swift action in order to avoid unpleasant consequences.
Entering a mine There may be people around you who will make promises they have no intention of keeping; you would be best to avoid them.
People trapped in the mine You need to be sensible and wise in order to extricate yourself from current difficulties.
Being a miner If you are a miner in real life, then this dream simply underlines your honesty and truthfulness, but if you are not a miner, it indicates that you have an unrealistic attitude to life that could cause you difficulties in the near future.

Mirages *see* **Oases**

Mirrors A mirror in a dream is a reminder of the fact that you are a good and kind person; it is extremely rare for anyone of bad character to dream of a mirror. It is also rare to see your own reflection in a mirror.

A cracked mirror You should continue to be helpful to others and not change the way you behave.

Being given a mirror This indicates that those around you are appreciative of what you do for them.

Monasteries For centuries, dreams of places of religious contemplation have come to symbolise an end to emotional conflicts and the beginning of a period of peace and calm. Seeing a monastery in a dream indicates that you are optimistic and accept the challenges of life with calm.

Being inside a monastery with someone If you are a man and in your dream you are with a woman you recognise, a woman will help you to solve your problems. If you are unmarried and you recognise the person, you are likely to find romance. If you are already married or in a relationship, the dream emphasises the strong bonds between you and your partner.

Eating inside a monastery If you are eating alone, this is an unmistakable sign of the end of bitter days. If you are with someone, it suggests friends and acquaintances will come to help you when you need them.

Sitting or standing inside a monastery This means a general transformation in your life for the better.

Writing inside a monastery If you are a writer by profession, this dream indicates success in your work. If you are presenting an application of any kind, it is a sure sign that there will be at least a partial positive response to it.

See also **Religious buildings**

Money If in your dream you see money thrown around you, it signifies a sudden breakthrough in your luck, usually for the better.

Picking up money You may receive a small gift or money from a friend.

Being given money If the money comes from your parents, it means that they continue to support you, and if it is from your children, it indicates that you are never likely to be in need. An employer giving you money signifies the possibility of doing well

at work and a rich person giving you money promises a successful business venture.
See also **Bribes, Buying, Coins, Treasure**

Money-lenders *see* **Loan companies**

Monkeys A monkey in a dream symbolises uncertainty and falsehood. If the monkey is sitting calmly, be wary of trusting those you do not know well. If it threatens you or is aggressive, it is a sign of uncertainty, but if you drive it away, then it is an indication that you will be successful in making the right decisions in the end.
A dead monkey You will soon see an end to a period of difficulty.

Moons
A crescent moon You have great spiritual depth.
A full moon This is a sign of good health or recovery from minor illnesses, and also happiness in general and the end to any family arguments.
A half moon You tend to be indecisive.
Travelling to the moon You are unlikely to suffer financial hardship.

Mosques *see* **Religious buildings**

Mothers This is an exceptionally favourable dream. If you see your mother in a dream, the problems you are experiencing are likely to come to an end quite soon. Her presence symbolises moral and spiritual support and healing.
Giving your mother a gift You will have a prosperous professional life.
Receiving a gift from your mother A wonderful dream, indicating protection from harm.

Mountains Seeing a mountain in a dream often indicates that you are underestimating your abilities and talents. With a little encouragement, you will be able to overcome this feeling and realise your ambitions. If you see a mountain in a place where it did not exist before, you are likely to be confronted with obstacles, but you will overcome them with wisdom and hard work.

Standing at the summit of a mountain You are nearing the fulfilment of your ambitions.
Falling from a mountain You have been fickle and hasty in judgement.
See also **Climbing**

Mourning Contrary to expectation, this dream indicates a new beginning in life.
Being in mourning You have great potential in you which, if properly utilised, will bring you happiness.
Other people in mourning If you recognise them, it is a sign of good luck. If you do not recognise them, you will do well if you continue to work hard.
Your family among the mourners A new and positive opportunity will open up to you shortly.
See also **Death, Funerals**

Mouths
A bleeding mouth You may encounter problems, possibly connected with the law.
A closed mouth You are unpredictable and not always truthful.
A normal and pleasant-looking mouth You enjoy friendship and good relationships with those around you.
A wide-open mouth You have a greedy and an argumentative nature.
Your own mouth If you are laughing, it could indicate some illegal activity. If you are unhappy or crying, it means that a compromise will end any misunderstandings or arguments.
See also **Lips, Teeth**

Mushrooms Mushrooms in a dream symbolise a sudden change or development for the better. Be encouraged to execute your plans.
Gathering mushrooms If you continue to work hard, you will reap the financial benefits.
Eating mushrooms Your approach to life is sometimes too hasty and could result in an unexpected setback.

N

Nails Seeing a single nail denotes a problem connected with your
job. A pile of nails suggests that you are in some doubt as to
how to deal with your present circumstances.
Hammering nails If you are hammering a nail into a door, it
indicates that, without realising it, you are blocking your own
progress. If you are hammering a nail into a box, it indicates that
you may experience family quarrels. However, pulling nails out
of anything suggests that you will soon experience a new
beginning.
See also **Hammers**

Nakedness Seeing yourself naked in a dream indicates that there
is a rough time ahead of you and you will be vulnerable to
difficulties, especially if you are in a poor neighbourhood. If
you manage to find something to wear or wrap yourself in,
your problems are likely to be short-lived. If you are in the
countryside or an attractive neighbourhood, it is likely to mean
that the difficulties will be caused by your not trying hard
enough.
Sleeping naked This can indicate that you have become involved
with a bad crowd. If you are sleeping on the pavement with just
a blanket to cover you, you are likely to experience a difficult
time but things will change for the better quite suddenly.
Seeing others naked Make sure that you have treated people
with the respect they deserve.
See also **Clothes, Undressing**

Narcotics *see* **Drugs**

Native country This dream only has significance if you live
abroad, in which case it indicates that you will experience a
sudden and very pleasant development in your life.

Necklaces A necklace in a dream generally indicates prosperity and
happiness. Seeing someone you know wearing a necklace
suggests a professional breakthrough. If you do not recognise
them, you are likely to receive a good offer related to your job.

A necklace lying on a table You are generally contented with your life.

Buying a necklace This indicates financial gain as long as you do not argue about the price. If so, it means that your obstinacy is likely to get in the way of progress.

Finding a necklace You have exceptional friends.

Losing a necklace Your behaviour may have been too reckless.

Receiving a necklace as a gift You are likely to receive a gift from someone you know.

Stealing a necklace This indicates that you must be careful not to snatch what you want.

See also **Jewellery, Pearls**

Needles A single needle indicates the possibility of an argument, perhaps even one connected with the law. A heap of needles indicates personal arguments, perhaps with your partner, which could end in an ugly scene.

Holding a needle You are determined to confront your detractors tactfully.

Pricking someone with a needle You are over-stressed and likely to act irrationally. Try to find ways to relax.

Threading a needle You will eventually tackle your problems to your own satisfaction. Holding a threaded needle indicates your readiness to embark on a new life.

See also **Sewing**

Nests A large nest with eggs or young but no parent bird indicates that you are able to live without depending on others. If the parent bird is present, you should think hard before embarking on any new plans.

An empty nest You will have to face future unhappiness.

Building a nest You will gain spiritually in the near future.

Smashing a bird's nest This dream indicates that you have an unforgiving nature and you should try to soften your approach.

A damaged nest Your reckless behaviour is quite likely to catch up with you.

See also **Eggs**

Nets Any kind of net in a dream indicates that you should try to be more realistic, otherwise you will not progress as quickly as you would like.

Getting entangled in a net Your angry and aggressive outbursts, especially in your personal relationships, have caused you problems – or soon will. Try to view situations with more calm and act accordingly. If you disentangle yourself, you will find ways of calming down and behaving more rationally.

News

Receiving pleasant news Promises may not always be what they seem.

Receiving bad news You will have to face a difficult situation alone.

See also **Results**

Noses

A small, turned-up nose This indicates petty, jealous arguments.

A large nose Harmony at home and possibly some financial gain are likely.

A bulbous nose You have a friendly and helpful attitude.

A hooked nose You have not been as generous as you should have been recently.

A bleeding nose You will come off worse in an argument, perhaps with your partner, or it may indicate a broken promise.

Nudity *see* **Nakedness**

Numbers Numbers in a dream usually relate to your specific situation, so you should consider the interpretations in the light of what is important to you at the time. They may appear on a wall, on clothes, on a vehicle or in any other place. Someone may suggest or call out a number or write it down, or you may murmur it to yourself. Interpretations of the numbers one to nine are given below. If it is a compound number, simplify it by adding the digits together until you reach a single number. For example, 849: $8 + 4 + 9 = 21; 2 + 1 = 3$.

One The number one can indicate loneliness or success and profit. If you have recently separated or argued with friends, then you are unlikely to be reconciled. If you have recently bought something in order to sell it, you are likely to make a modest profit, although if you have a partner in the deal, you may expect a loss.

Two Disagreements, arguments and obstacles are symbolised by the number two. If you are planning to try to solve a dispute or intervene on behalf of someone else, consider whether this is a good time to take such action. Postpone business deals for a week and avoid family gatherings that might involve confrontation.

Three Reconciliation of broken friendships is indicated by the number three. There are also chances to meet a new friend. If someone writes this figure in front of you or on your clothes, you could receive an expensive present. If you murmur it, you will achieve a minor goal in three days or three weeks. If you have been ill, you'll soon recover.

Four Stability, security and success in modest projects are indicated by dreaming of the number four. It will bring good luck to farmers or workers.

Five Five helps you to understand the reasons for any difficulties or setbacks you have been experiencing, as you are likely to receive a hint of the person who is causing your problems after you have seen five in the dream. If your problems are of your own making, the dream will also make that clear.

Six This chiefly relates to family developments. If you have misunderstandings with your parents or partner, they are likely to be resolved to everyone's satisfaction. Reunions with family members can also be indicated by dreaming of six. If you are alone, you should seek a reunion with your family, as it is likely to be to your benefit.

Seven Good things follow dreaming of seven and you may want to celebrate. Life is going to improve. Exam results or the answers to queries are likely to be good. Business deals are likely to go well. Reunions are possible for those who have been separated. Gamblers and financial speculators, however, can expect losses.

Eight This figure chiefly deals with financial activities. The unemployed should experience an offer within the next couple of months. Those troubled by financial difficulties may find that things improve. If someone owes you money, you are likely to receive at least half of it very soon.

Nine Uncertainty, loss and ill-health are related to the figure nine in a dream. Buying or selling property or business deals in general should be avoided for a couple of weeks at least. Try to avoid intervening in a family argument or setting out on a long journey. A short journey should not be affected.

Nuns Truth, modesty and spiritual values are indicated by dreaming of a nun.

A nun passes you There is likely to be an end to family arguments.

Questioning a nun If she answers you, it indicates a good business or work opportunity. If she refuses to answer you, be more cautious in your dealings at work or connected with finances over the next month.

Quarrelling with a nun Things will not go well over the next few weeks.

Giving something to a nun You are pleased with what you have achieved. If you are ill, you can expect a cure.

Nurses A nurse at work symbolises help for you which could enhance your living standards. A nurse telling you that you will recover means that your difficulties will be solved gradually. If the nurse tells you in your dream that you are ill when in fact you are healthy, it means that if things get worse for you, it is likely to be your own fault. If the nurse says you are in good health, you will have to work hard in life.

Being a nurse An advantageous business deal is indicated here. If you are treating others, it is an indication of happiness at home.

See also **Doctors, Hospitals, Illness**

Oars A single oar denotes that good advice will come when you need it, while a pair of oars suggests that you will have all the support you need. Someone giving you oars has a similar significance.

Holding oars If you are holding them, you are doing things well in your life. However, if the oars are being held by other people, you may be allowing others to be too influential and failing to make your own decisions.

Broken oars You may encounter petty obstacles. If you break oars in dream, it means that you are restless and may be unreliable.

Rowing with oars If you are using them easily, things will go well for you, but if you are finding difficulty with them, things may start to go wrong.

See also **Boats**

Oases An oasis, whether seen from close up or at a distance, offers sanctuary from your problems, and if you are at the oasis, family problems in particular will improve. However, if the oasis turns out to be a mirage or if you see people arguing or fighting there, then the opposite interpretation comes into play.

See also **Deserts**

Oceans

A calm, clear ocean You are likely to enjoy success in love, perhaps with a person older than you.

A ship on the ocean Your financial circumstances will improve.

A stormy ocean This indicates that you should be careful of what is ahead and act cautiously. If you are trying to help someone, it indicates that you like to be thought helpful and kind.

Swimming in an ocean You think you can do anything, but you should exercise caution, especially where your emotions are concerned.

See also **Sailing, Water**

Ointment An improvement in your health is likely if you have been suffering from any minor problems.

Old age Old age in a dream generally indicates a long and healthy life, so if you see yourself as an old person, it is a good sign. If you are young and are engaged in pleasant conversation with elderly people, you may have to work hard but you are likely to do well.

Onions Grief and unhappiness are indicated by dreaming of onions, perhaps as a result of a sad development within the family.
Buying onions Petty misunderstandings could lead to serious arguments if the situation is not handled with sensitivity.
Harvesting onions You must take responsibility for the difficult circumstances in which you find yourself.
Peeling onions Continuous arguments will lead to serious unhappiness if you do not take steps to alter the situation and find a resolution to the difficulties.
Rotten onions Your present difficulties are likely to be overcome.

Orange *see* **Colour**

Oranges Oranges in a dream can have a variety of meanings depending on the circumstances. Generally, they symbolise a change, not necessarily for the better.
A basket of oranges A dramatic change is indicated, which may be good or bad, but if you trample the fruit then you will negate any bad effects.
Eating oranges Problems are in store, perhaps even holding legal implications. If you are eating oranges with your partner, try to avoid misunderstandings that could become serious.
Buying oranges This is an indication of health problems.
Being offered oranges Financial difficulties or loss of some kind are indicated by this dream.
Orange trees You may cheat or be cheated by someone you love.

Orchids Orchids in a dream are a symbol of the strong bonds of friendship or married commitment.
Someone you recognise offers you orchids You are likely to cement a true and lasting friendship with them. If it is your partner, your relationship will be strong and enduring. If any of your children presents them to you, it indicates that their love and respect for you.
A field full of orchids The intervention of friends will bring an end to hardships.

Orders

Receiving an order This dream is likely to signify a change in your life, possibly sudden.

Orphans If you know the orphan and they appear to be happy, you can expect a good period to follow for you, but if they appear unhappy, the time ahead is likely to be difficult. If someone tells you that the child in front of you is an orphan, you can expect a separation of some kind in your life, although not necessarily a permanent one.
Being an orphan You have not been utilising your talents and abilities to the full. Think about how best you can achieve your potential.

Ostriches An ostrich symbolises hypocrisy, worries and difficulties. If it is running, it indicates dubious friends. If standing still, it suggests that if you cannot achieve your goals it is because of your own laziness.
A flock of ostriches Difficulties will result from your own extravagance.
A dead ostrich You will soon come to the end of the difficulties you have been suffering.

Owls Dreaming of an owl is only considered auspicious if the bird is seen from a distance, in which case it is a sign of sagacity. However, if the bird is close to you, it indicates ill-health in the family, especially if it is hooting.
Several owls around you You are likely to experience severe difficulties of some kind.
A dead owl A bad period is coming to an end.

P

Pain Any form of pain or illness in a dream symbolises a temporary setback in life. Fever in a dream, however, generally has an organic origin (see page 9) and is not significant.

Feeling pain Aching muscles can be an indication of a serious forthcoming argument, either at work or with your partner. Pain in the ears denotes that you should listen more carefully to constructive criticism. Pain in the eyes reflects the fact that you are not ready to face challenges.

Seeing someone in pain This should serve as a warning to take great care in your everyday affairs. If the person is a relative, be particularly careful, as there is the possibility of an accident.

Painters Seeing a painter at work in a dream symbolises your creative ability and talents in completing projects. If the painter has finished a piece of work, take it as encouragement to continue with what you are working on. If the painter speaks to you, you will require patience to achieve your latest project.

Being a painter You will arrive at your goals only if you continue to make a serious effort.

Palaces Seeing a palace in the distance underlines the fact that you are being too overbearing in your attitude to others. If you are near the palace, this is a warning against false, insincere friends.

Being inside a palace An empty palace signifies that someone around you may have ulterior motives in courting your friendship. If the palace is full, it signifies generous help from a friend.

A ruler in a palace This dream marks the beginning of a prosperous life, brought about through your own efforts.

See also **Kings, Mansions, Queens**

Parrots Parrots in flight indicate that you are confused and need rest. A single parrot, either flying or perched on a tree, suggests uncertainty in your plans.

A parrot speaks to you You have an awkward and illogical approach to life.

A caged parrot Your life may be unfruitful unless you seek support and help from people who have more knowledge than you.

A dead parrot You will have peace of mind, temporarily at least.

Parties *see* **Celebrations**

Partridges A single partridge at a distance means modest financial gains, while if it is closer it indicates general prosperity.
A flock of partridges Whether they are on the ground or in the air, partridges in large numbers symbolise an unexpected loss or difficulties.
A dead partridge You will experience a general recovery.

Passports Success in business or romance is indicated by a dream featuring a passport. Even if the passport is not yours, it is a sign that you should proceed with your projects. Seeing your own passport is a sign of a beneficial trip. If you are holding the passport in your hand, you are likely to have a pleasant surprise in store over the next few months.
Applying for a passport This indicates success in business or at work. If you are handed your passport by an official, you can look forward to promotion or profit. Being refused a passport means you should rethink your next move.
Losing your passport Misplacing, forgetting or losing your passport indicates that there are flaws in your plans. If your passport is taken away from you, take particular care to review what you are planning.

Peaches Peaches symbolise good health, a stable marriage and success at work. A tree loaded with ripe peaches indicates a strong degree of unity within the family.
Eating, buying or selling peaches This speaks of good health, happiness in the family and a stable married life.
Being offered peaches Your family and friends will be generous towards you.
Picking peaches You attach a strong degree of importance to your health.

Peacocks False pride and dishonesty are indicated by seeing a peacock with its tail fanned out. If it turns around, it suggests that you will search for fame through any means. If the peacock is with a peahen, it indicates arguments with your spouse.
A flying peacock or peahen You cannot realise your goals.

Pearls If you see a single pearl, it denotes exceptionally good health. Several pearls are a sign that you are likely to come into money, perhaps through an inheritance.

A pearl on a chain You will meet someone and fall in love. If you are wearing the pearl, it indicates a gift from a friend or admirer.

A string of pearls You will be successful in business. If you are wearing it, that success is likely to be imminent.

Giving pearls If you give pearls to your lover, it indicates that you will have a happily married life together.

Receiving pearls from anyone You get on well with those around you.

Buying pearls You may suffer a sudden financial loss, or break up with a business partner.

Selling pearls You are experiencing some financial difficulties.

See also **Jewellery, Necklaces**

Pelicans One or more pelicans swimming means you can have confidence in your friends. A pelican near you suggests assistance in reaching your goals.

Feeding a pelican You are compassionate towards those less fortunate than yourself.

A dead pelican There will be some sort of misunderstanding in your life.

Peppers Fresh peppers are a good sign in a dream as they suggest good health, financial gain and promotion. Rotten peppers mean temporary problems.

Buying peppers Your ambitions will soon be realised.

Eating peppers This is a sign of good health.

Growing peppers A successful business or good opportunities at work are suggested by this dream.

Harvesting peppers You are likely to have opportunities for success or promotion at work or a new employment offer.

Selling peppers You will continue to get on well with those around you.

Pharmacies Seeing a pharmacy in a dream, whether it is close by or in the distance, is an indication of possible illness in the near future. If you are inside, family arguments, perhaps with your partner, are likely to make things difficult for you at home.

Buying medicine in a pharmacy This indicates that you are likely to find a resolution to your health problems or to problems at home. However, if you leave the pharmacy empty-handed, you are likely to have difficulties for some time to come.
See also **Medicine**

Pictures A single picture reflects a few current problems as a result of the fact that other people do not list your needs among their priorities. The greater the number of pictures, the more difficulties you are likely to have as a result.
Buying and selling pictures You are looking for a way forward in life which does not involve being dishonest or dealing with dishonest people.
Being given a picture You will discover the reasons why you are failing to do as well as you would hope. If you are given one picture, a friend will help you in this, while if you are given several pictures, then you are likely to have more than one supporter.

Pigeons A pigeon indicates affection and kindness towards you from those around you, and if it is in flight, it indicates good news.
A dead pigeon This can mean financial loss.
Feeding pigeons You can expect to fulfil most of your ambitions.
A flock of pigeons in flight A visit from a friend or member of your family is indicated.
A pair of pigeons This means a happy married life.
A wounded pigeon You have a tendency to be irresponsible.

Pigs A pig in a dream symbolises loss or bad luck. If you are planning a journey, an interview or a business venture, try to postpone it for a week or so. If you see two pigs in the dream, jealousy may cause others to act against you.
Pigs in a pen You may be involved in some legal proceedings.

Pilgrimages This dream denotes good luck, happiness, good health and continued success at work. It also underlines the importance you attach to spiritual values.
Going on a pilgrimage Beginning a journey on a pilgrimage suggests you will have good luck over the next few months. If you are alone, it suggest you will have to be sensible and take

advantage of the opportunities which open up to you. If you are with others, you will have the benefit of sound advice from friends.

Visiting a holy shrine Approaching a shrine indicates that you will have success and happiness in all areas of your life. Being inside a shrine foretells success and underlines the importance of your spiritual life.

Pilots Dreaming of a pilot is generally an auspicious dream.

Piloting an aeroplane This is an exceptionally good dream indicating that you have abilities or perhaps hidden talents that can be exploited to your considerable advantage.

Standing close to or talking to the pilot This dream suggests the possibility of moving away from any difficulties you have recently experienced.

See also **Aeroplanes**

Pimples *see* **Acne**

Pipes *see* **Cigarettes**

Pirates A pirate is a symbol of danger and risks. Seeing one on a ship denotes you are likely to embark on a risky enterprise which is not likely to turn out well for you. Be cautious and seek professional advice where appropriate. If the pirate appears on land, be careful in your choice of friends.

Being a pirate You may have already taken unacceptable risks or made decisions which you knew were not in everyone's best interests. Especially if the scene is aggressive, you would do well to reconsider some of your recent actions.

Planes *see* **Aeroplanes**

Ploughs A plough symbolises your need to follow a traditional way of life and underlines the likelihood of a happy married life.

You are ploughing If you are alone, you will do well through your own hard work. If you are being helped by someone, you will receive help from your relatives when you need it. If you have just finished ploughing, you can expect a comfortable, if not affluent, and contented life.

Seeing someone ploughing You will have a happy married life.

Plums A plate full of plums signifies good health, but if they are
rotten, it indicates illness within the family.
  Buying plums A misunderstanding in the family is possible.
  Picking plums You may have been behaving in an obstinate
  way. Try to be more tolerant of the opinions of others.
  Selling plums You will recover from illness.

Poetry
  Reading poetry This dream suggests a well-earned rest.
  Writing poetry You have a realistic and serious approach to life.
  Correcting or rewriting a poem You are able to change your
  lifestyle if you wish.
  Listening to poetry Contentment or spiritual growth are
  indicated by this dream, depending on the nature of the poetry
  being read.

Poison Poison in any form foretells quarrels with friends. If you are
holding it in your hand, it can indicate serious arguments with
your partner.
  Taking poison Be particularly careful and do not take any risks.
  If you are over-stressed, take positive steps to remedy the
  situation by seeking help from friends or professionals or finding
  ways to relax.

Police officers Seeing a police officer in a dream is a sign that you
will receive help and support from friends or relatives.
  Being a police officer Things are going well for you and the
  prospects are good.
  Receiving an offer of help from a police officer You are likely
  to receive all the help you need to fulfil your plans and you
  should consider this a good sign to go ahead with any business
  deals or other arrangements. If you are unemployed, your
  prospects will improve. If you are unhappy, things are likely to
  get better.
  Arguing with a police officer You have some sorting out to do
  but it should end up for the best.

Polygamy If you practise or discuss polygamy in a dream, this is
considered an unfavourable omen.

Committing polygamy Arguments at home and disagreements or misunderstandings which could become serious are indicated by this dream.

Pomegranates This is a propitious dream indicating good things. A plate or basket of the fruit is a sign of wealth.
Eating pomegranates This dream indicates a long and healthy life.
Offering or receiving pomegranates Your life will be successful in almost all spheres.
Buying pomegranates You will have a successful marriage and personal relationships.
Picking pomegranates Your life is likely to be unique and you will not suffer from financial hardship.

Poppies Dreaming of poppies in a field means that you are living in a world of falsehood and deceit.
Being offered poppies You are likely to be offered an opportunity to act immorally or even illegally and should be aware that you will have to expect appropriate consequences.
Touching a poppy You will shortly suffer a period of ill-health unless you take particular care of yourself.

Porters Seeing a porter carrying a load indicates business or employment problems and resultant financial hardship.
Being a porter You may be confused as to what your next step should be. If someone offers you luggage to carry, you will find help to resolve your indecision.
An idle porter This dream indicates a period of idleness.

Potatoes Potatoes in a dream, however they appear, generally indicate financial difficulties.
A field of unharvested potatoes You are uncertain about the future.
Throwing away potatoes You will experience an amelioration of your problems.

Praise
Receiving praise If you dream that someone is praising you, take this as a sign of encouragement.

Prayers Prayers in a dream indicate gratitude, success, happiness and a modest financial standing.

You are praying If you are alone in a place of worship, you are happy with your life and your spiritual development. If you are with others, you are likely to be successful in life. If you are praying alone at home, your house will remain a happy place to live. If you are with other family members, you can expect your life to continue to be happy.

Seeing others praying If your parents are praying, it indicates that you are likely to have a happy married life, whether or not you are married at the time. If your friends are praying, it denotes sincere friendship.

See also **Religious buildings**

Pregnancy This dream only has significance if you are not a pregnant woman in real life.

You are pregnant If you are unmarried, this dream suggests that you may have difficulties if you continue to be lazy; if you are married, it may be your partner who is idle. If you are married and already have children, you may experience a financial setback or bout of illness in the family. If you are divorced or separated, there could be work problems in store for you. If you are unemployed, the prospects will not improve for some time. However, if you are elderly, it indicates that your life will be happy and you will not have to do without anything you really want.

Someone else is pregnant Plan your moves carefully and make sure you are on good terms with those around you.

Preserves *see* **Jam**

Prisons Seeing a prison in a dream suggests that things are going to improve for you and you will find the energy and talent to start a constructive project.

Seeing people in prison Your friends will offer their help and support when needed. If there is only one person behind bars, however, there may be a delay in getting the support you need.

Being in prison If you are with friends, you will be busy for the foreseeable future, but if you are alone it is a sign of disappointment.

Profanity *see* **Swearing**

Prophets The presence of a prophet in your dream is a very positive indication. If you are ill, you are likely to recover. If you are unemployed or having difficulties at work, things will improve. In general, you are well regarded by those around you. If the prophet appears to be pleased with you, a sudden change for the better is indicated.
A prophet gives you something This indicates the beginning of your search for a more spiritual dimension to your life.

Proposals of marriage If a married person proposes in a dream, or if an unmarried person proposes to a married person, it signifies that they are not taking their responsibilities sufficiently seriously, either in relationships or at work, and that their view of life is unrealistic. If an unmarried person proposes to another unmarried person, however, financial improvements or other improvements in your life are indicated.
See also **Marriage, Polygamy, Remarriage**

Prostitutes Dreaming of a prostitute means that you should not place too much confidence in your friends unless you are very sure of their honesty. If the prostitute approaches you, be careful with your health. If you have sex with the prostitute, the indications are more serious.
Being a prostitute This dream is generally unfavourable and signifies arguments with your partner, family, friends or parents.

Punishment
Receiving a punishment Be careful in your dealings with those you do not know well. You may receive bad news at work or argue with your employer.

Purses Whether empty or full, a purse is a lucky omen as it signifies gain through your own hard work. If it is full, the advantages will come with less effort.
Buying a purse You intend to work hard.
Finding a purse Your friends and family will always help you when you need them.
Losing a purse You have an unrealistic approach to life.

Pyramids A pyramid is a successful image in a dream. If you are near the pyramid, it indicates a happy and productive period in your life. If it is in the distance, there will be work to be done but it will be worth it.

*A **damaged** **pyramid*** This dream generally indicates a setback.

Falling from a pyramid If this happens in your dream, it is an indication that you are being too careless.

Standing on or in a pyramid A rare dream, this indicates business, financial or work success.

Q

Quarries

An empty quarry This dream indicates hardships, possibly caused by legal problems. If people are working there, especially if you recognise any of them, then the legal implications become stronger.

Falling into a quarry Those people whom you consider to beyour friends may not turn out to have your best interests at heart. However, if you manage to clamber out of the quarry, you will get out of your difficulties on your own.

Working in a quarry This dream is an indication of your troubles in life and signifies that your antisocial attitude and activities will cause you problems.

Queens
A queen ornately dressed is an indication of financial problems, possibly severe. If she is with friends or officials, your problems are likely to be of your own making. If she is at a party, help for you is unlikely to be forthcoming. The more splendid the scene, the more likely the difficulties are to be serious, although the presence of a king in the dream neutralises the effect.

Being a queen Revenge or malice may be in your mind. You would be advised to change your attitude.

See also **Kings, Palaces**

Questions
Asking questions indicates that you want to find a good path through life.

Questioning a lawyer or legal representative It is likely that you are looking to move away from illegal or immoral activities.

Questioning a priest or holy person You have strong religious inclinations.

Asking questions of work colleagues You have a strong spiritual element in your make-up.

Being asked questions Help and support are indicated by being asked questions by your parents or people you know. If you are asked questions by a legal official, you should take it as advice to make sure you have proper answers in real life to any difficult questions you may be asked.

Quicksand If you are far away from the quicksand, take care in financial dealings. If you are near, take especial care of your health.

Falling into quicksand If you do not sink, you may experience a temporary setback at work or in your financial status. If you are able to save yourself, you will be successful in business. If someone helps to pull you out, your friends will be similarly supportive in life.

Quiz games Playing any kind of quiz or general knowledge game indicates that opportunities will open up to you very soon.

R

Rabbis A rabbi symbolises truth and decency. If the rabbi is conducting a religious meeting, it underlines your own feelings of the importance of truth in life.

Being a rabbi A new and fruitful life will begin soon.

A rabbi gives you something You will have a happy life.

Speaking with a rabbi If the rabbi is speaking casually with people, you are likely to receive consolation for your difficulties. If he or she speaks with you, your health will improve if you have been having problems, or will remain good.

Rabbits

A running rabbit You have the ability to make swift decisions.

A rabbit lying down You have a chance to prove your abilities if you choose to take it.

Feeding a rabbit This dream indicates financial gain.

Racing Unless you are a sportsperson, this dream generally indicates an uncertain life marked by confrontation, especially if you enter and lose a race. For people heavily involved in sports, it is a good sign to dream of participating in a race, as it indicates continued good health and success.

Rage *see* **Anger**

Rain Light showers symbolise a new beginning, the end to minor worries and even an unexpected meeting with someone who will be influential in your life. Torrential rain symbolises financial setbacks due to faulty planning or unreliable associates. If this leads to floods, it suggests you should be especially cautious with regard to your business partners.

Standing in the rain If you are soaking wet, you will have to work hard to make a success of a small project. If you have an umbrella or if the rain does not seem to make you wet, you will succeed in whatever you are planning.

Raspberries This fruit is usually associated with disappointments or arguments.

Eating or buying raspberries A disappointment or loss of some kind is indicated in your life.

Being given raspberries Be warned that potentially serious misunderstandings are likely to occur in your family if you do not make strenuous efforts to overcome them.

Picking raspberries Your behaviour may have been too rash and reckless. Try to follow a more modest path and be prepared to accept responsibility for your decisions and actions.

Rotten raspberries There are likely to be disappointments for those in love if they have had this dream.

Rats Several rats in a dream indicate greed.

Rats in or around a kitchen You may experience the end of your constructive aims in life unless you change your course.

Rats near the bedroom Jealousy and animosity are indicated.

Chasing or killing rats You will eventually gain the upper hand.

Recovering from illness If you are healthy, this is generally a sign that you will retain your health. However, if you are actually ill and you dream of recovering, you should pay more attention to looking after yourself rather than just expecting to get better without any effort.
See also **Hospitals**

Religious buildings Any building where religious ceremonies are carried out, such as a cathedral, church, mosque, synagogue or temple, is a place where people seek understanding, peace, happiness, forgiveness of sins and guidance from heaven, so any dream involving a religious building is the best possible dream from a spiritual point of view.

Being inside a religious building Your prayers have been answered and you have achieved calm, tranquillity and spiritual awareness.

Walking towards a religious building This is a wonderful dream, which indicates that you want to exchange your material gains for spiritual wealth. It also reflects your intentions to disassociate yourself from undesirable companions and lead a decent life.
See also **Monasteries, Prayers**

Remarriage If a widow or widower dreams of remarrying someone who has not been married or who is also a widow or widower, that is a sign of a long and happy life. If someone who is actually married dreams of remarrying, it indicates that their relationship with their partner may be unstable and need attention. If you dream of remarrying your ex-partner, it is often a sign that you are feeling extremely unhappy and stressed and you would benefit from positive action to change your life for the better.
See also **Marriage, Proposals of marriage**

Restaurants Just seeing a restaurant, whether close by or at a distance, indicates an unhappy life, and perhaps a lonely one.
Entering a restaurant If it is busy, it suggests you will have a busy and profitable schedule. If the restaurant is empty, it denotes that some of your friends are unreliable and will make promises they have no intention of keeping.
Owning a restaurant Good days are not far away.
See also **Eating**

Results Awaiting any kind of result in a dream symbolises anxiety and stress. If it is the result of an examination or test in the dream, you are likely to be over-stressed about something that is happening to you at the moment.
Receiving a result If the dream suggests a negative response, then the real one is likely to be positive.

Reunions A reunion with old friends, business partners or family members symbolises happiness, success at work, increased energy and an end to arguments or misunderstandings. However, any anger or aggressive behaviour at the reunion will have a negative connotation.
Going to a reunion If you go to a reunion with old friends you have not seen for some time, it indicates encouragement and renewed vigour to begin a new phase in your life. If it is a reunion with old school friends, you can expect continued good health and perhaps a promotion or advancement at work. If you have a reunion with your former business colleagues, it indicates financial and moral support to start a business or set off on a new employment direction. A reunion with family suggests the resolution of an argument. If you are offered a gift, it is a sure sign of success.

Riding Riding an animal symbolises money, friends, good health
and happy relationships. If you are riding with your lover or
partner, you will have a happy married life.
Riding a camel A dromedary with one hump indicates a short
journey which may be advantageous. A Bactrian camel indicates
financial gain, perhaps through inheritance.
Riding a donkey or mule Influential people will be helpful to
you.
Riding a horse This indicates that you will do well at work.
Seeing others riding This is a lucky sign indicating help and
support when you need it.

Rings Giving a ring to someone you love who also loves you
indicates a happy relationship. If your love is unrequired,
however, then the relationship is likely to break up and that
person will not make a happy marriage.
Finding a ring You will have a happy married life.
Losing or breaking your wedding ring Unnecessary arguments
are likely to cause friction between you and your partner.
See also **Jewellery**

Rivers A clear and smooth-flowing river in a dream symbolises true
love. If the river has an uneven flow with rocks on the bed, you
could encounter obstacles in your path but you should be able to
overcome them if you act sensibly. If the river is dirty or very
fast-flowing, you may have more problems than you had
anticipated. If you touch the dirty water or swim in it, you are
wasting your time on unrealistic projects.
A river suddenly flows near your house A sudden change in
your life will benefit you.
A river in flood This dream is a warning to refrain from any
risky undertakings. If you see property being destroyed, you
should be thoughtful and considerate in order to avoid problems.
Swimming in a river You will continue to be happy.
See also **Floods and flooding, Swimming, Water**

Roads
A straight, wide road There is an easy path to what you want
to achieve.
A narrow, gravelled road You are experiencing difficulties at
the moment.

A narrow, winding road You will have a pleasant surprise in the near future.

A cobbled road Whether it is narrow or wide, straight or winding, such a dream promises positive results for hard work.
See also **Driving, Travelling**

Robbers *see* **Criminals**

Robbery Any form of robbery indicates nervous behaviour and lack of self-control.

Being robbed You are lacking in self-control, which may cause you problems.

Participating in a robbery This dream suggests that you may be thinking about doing something which you know is wrong, or you may even have plans to commit an illegal act.

Seeing a robbery You are over-stressed.

Rocks Rocks signify obstacles and problems. If they are in your way while riding, walking or driving, you are likely to be confronted with obstacles which are not of your own making. If you manage to avoid them and continue your journey, your setbacks will be short-lived. If you are not able to get past the obstruction, then you will have to work harder and be wise in order to proceed.

Climbing a huge rock You have the potential to start on a new project or change your course in life without support, if necessary.

Falling from a rock You need to be realistic as your projects could be too extravagant.

Roofs Any roof in a dream symbolises protection from harm or unexpected help to overcome problems.

Building a roof You are likely to do better at work, or to embark on a successful business venture, especially if you have just completed the roof.

A collapsed roof Plan more carefully if you want to avoid difficulties.

Standing under a roof You have the protection of reliable friends.

Ropes Seeing a rope lying on the ground, hanging, or in a coil is a warning to be careful not to make minor mistakes.
Being tied with a rope Bad planning is likely to result in serious setbacks or obstacles to your progress. You may be too stressed to be able to work efficiently. Take advice or ask for professional help, if necessary. If you manage to free yourself, it is a good sign that you will feel better very shortly.
Tying someone with a rope You are feeling angry and aggressive. Try to relax and be calmer.
See also **Knots**

Roses True love and deep affection are symbolised by a rose of any colour in a dream. If you are presented with roses by the person you love, it suggests an early marriage or, if you are already married, a happy life together.
Buying roses This indicates a prosperous business deal or good employment prospects.
Cutting roses You are likely to be celebrating the successful outcome of a project.

Rowing *see* **Oars**

Rugs *see* **Carpets**

Rulers *see* **Kings, Palaces, Queens**

Running If you are running away from danger, it underlines your intelligence. If you are running to find something, it denotes your constructive attitude. If you are running to indulge in something bad or even illegal, it is an indication of uncertainty and even failure. If you are running for exercise, it denotes a healthy life, but if you fall while you are running it indicates that you need to be more careful.
Other people running This is an encouraging sign that you should continue with what you are doing. Seeing a criminal running is a sign to be careful in your choice of friends.
See also **Racing, Travelling**

S

Sabres *see* **Swords**

Sacks
> *A small sack tied at the top* You are likely to receive a pleasant surprise or a positive response to a request.
> *A large, closed sack* A fruitful proposal is indicated.
> *An open sack filled with useful objects* If the sack is small, you will receive a small gift or modest help. If the sack is large, the dream indicates that you will have help and support from dependable friends to reach your goals.
> *An open, empty sack* You will have to work hard to achieve your ambitions.
> *Being given a sack of valuables* Do not depend too much on other people's help since it will dissuade you from being independent.
> *See also* **Bags**

Saddles Hard work, patience and dislike of pomposity are indicated by dreaming of a saddle.
> *A saddle on a horse* This indicates a fruitful journey.
> *Making or repairing a saddle* This dream underlines the fact that you are honest and contented with what you have.
> *See also* **Horses, Riding**

Safes
> *A closed safe* You have a tendency towards a miserly nature without compassion and you would do better to be more open and generous.
> *An open safe* If it contains valuables, this dream symbolises your indifference to life, while an empty safe denotes your willingness to go to any extreme to get what you want.
> *A safe that has been robbed* An unhappy and perhaps isolated period may be in store for you.

Sailing Sailing symbolises success and prosperity in general and also a happy family life.
> *You are sailing* If you are in a small boat, it denotes success in business. If the boat is a large one in full sail, it is a general

symbol of prosperity. If you are alone, then you are likely to realise your ambitions without help. If your family are with you, you will have a happy married life and achieve your goals. **Others are sailing** Continue with your efforts and you will be successful.
See also **Boats, Oceans, Ships**

Saints This is a wonderful dream symbolising truth and justice, an end to problems and a life with a strong spiritual element. It is commonly accepted that those dreaming of saints should not relate their dream to other people. If the saint appears to bless you, you will be particularly fortunate. If the saint gives you something or talks to you, you will be protected from harm.

Salt Whether in a packet or jar or on a plate, salt indicates that help will soon come to solve your problems.
Being offered salt If it is by someone you recognise, that person will come to your support when you need it. If you do not recognise them, you will shortly meet someone who will be helpful to you.
Offering salt This denotes your good character.
Buying salt Buying salt indicates welcome guests.
Selling salt You could experience minor family difficulties.

Sand Plan your projects carefully or you will experience obstacles and difficulties; try to avoid major purchases or sales for a couple of weeks. Consider the advantages and disadvantages of any work-related choices very carefully before you make any decisions.
Being surrounded by sand Further difficulties will come your way.
See also **Deserts, Oases, Seashores**

Schools Any type of school symbolises opportunities to start a new life, perhaps with the help and support of friends and family. If there are students in the school, it is a positive sign that you should start planning. If the students are in the school playground or grounds, it is an indication of relief from worries.
Being at school Finding yourself back at school studying one of your favourite subjects is a good sign of bright prospects in life. Being spoken to by one of your teachers indicates that you will receive help to make a good start in life.

A nursery school If the school is full of very young children, your ambitions will soon be realised. An empty and deserted school, however, denotes that your plans may be unrealistic and you should review them before proceeding further.
See also **Teachers**

Scissors A married person dreaming of scissors can indicate an argument with their partner, which could have implications for the atmosphere in the house for some time to come.
Threatening someone with scissors This is a sign of stress.
Using scissors Using scissors for a constructive purpose indicates that you will fulfil your plans but if you are using them to destroy something, you may have a destructive streak.

Seashores If, in your dreams, you see a seashore either close to you or in the distance, this means you have to steel yourself to begin a constructive future. You may be feeling hopeless about your circumstances but it is up to you to change the situation.
Being on the seashore If you are standing or sitting idly, you have not yet realised or even discovered your potential.
Searching for something on the seashore You are beginning to take constructive steps.
Sleeping on a shore You have feelings of uncertainty. Stand up and face the challenges with courage and honesty.

Selling
Selling an animal This gives the indication that you would be prepared to do anything to get what you want.
Selling a house or property for business reasons This suggests financial profit at work, or perhaps a promotion.
Selling something because you need money A temporary financial setback is indicated.
See also **individual items being sold**

Sewing
You are sewing You have a constructive approach to problem-solving.
Other people sewing You should be encouraged to search for solutions to your problems.
See also **Needles, Tailors**

Sharpening If you are sharpening any object in your dream, you are likely to embark on an ambitious project, which will demand a lot of hard work but will be successful in the end.
Sharpening a weapon Sharpening an offensive object with criminal or destructive intentions is a representation of some bad intentions you may have in real life.
See also **Daggers, Knives, Swords, Weapons**

Sheep
A lamb You have grateful children.
Grazing sheep These are an indication of inner peace coming after a stormy period, largely as a result of your own honesty.
Stroking sheep You are generally contented with your life.
Walking among sheep Your friends will not disappoint you.

Shepherds A shepherd standing around idly suggests irresponsibility, but if they are looking after their flock, it suggests a few days of hectic activity.
Being a shepherd Personal and domestic happiness are indicated by this dream. If you are surrounded by your sheep, you are likely to get on well with most people.

Shields A shield in a dream is a sign of encouragement and hope.
Holding a shield You have made a decision to try your hand at a project you have been considering, or perhaps your financial circumstances will improve or problems be resolved.

Ships
A passenger ship If it is sailing smoothly, this signifies a contented family life, whereas if it is on a stormy sea, it is an indication of impending arguments or unhappiness.
A cargo ship This dream relates to business or work in a similar way to a passenger ship (above).
A naval ship Whatever the circumstances, this is a suggestion of uncertainty due to your own lack of understanding.
Being on a ship If the ship is sailing smoothly, this dream indicates that things will go well for you for the foreseeable future. If the ship is in stormy waters, you need to take extra care with your life.
See also **Boats, Oceans, Sailing, Shipwrecks, Sinking**

Shipwrecks If you dream of a shipwreck, any difficulties you encounter are likely to be the result of your own mismanagement and irresponsibility. If the ship has sunk completely below the water, it is a strong warning to adopt a new strategy at work. A shipwreck on the coast suggests financial loss.

Being shipwrecked If you are under the water, you may find you need a complete change in your job. If you are on the shore, you will need to make extreme efforts to make things go well at work but you are most likely to succeed.

See also **Boats, Drowning, Ships**

Shirts Shirts that you see in dreams have different meanings according to their colour.

A clean, brightly coloured shirt This dream indicates that your life will improve through your own efforts.

A multi-coloured shirt This indicates an indecisiveness on your part.

A torn shirt Jealousy is making its presence felt in your life.

Wearing a shirt Dark-coloured clothes tend to indicate that you have difficulty planning or understanding the bare necessities in life. If you are wearing a black shirt, you may not be as frank as you claim.

Buying a shirt Buying a brightly coloured shirt denotes your desire to improve your way of life. Buying a black shirt shows that you have regrets about your own shortcomings.

Shoes

Worn-out shoes You will have a meeting with friends you have not seen for some time.

Being surrounded by new shoes This dream is a sign of a long and useless journey.

Putting on your shoes You will make new efforts to compensate for previous failures.

Removing your shoes You are likely to enjoy a hard-earned rest quite soon.

Shopkeepers A grocer or shopkeeper in a dream denotes hard work and even risks in life.

Receiving news from a shopkeeper If they give you good news, you should continue to persevere and work hard in life to achieve your goals; if you know the person, the indication is even more promising. If they give you bad news, however, you are likely to encounter problems which will require resolution.

Quarrelling with a shopkeeper If you know the person, you are quite careful and likely to be successful at work. If you do not know them, you are not a risk-taker in life.

See also **Bakers, Butchers, Selling, Shops**

Shops The significance of a shop in a dream depends on the type of business.

A butcher's shop An angry confrontation is likely.

A cake or sweet shop A happy reunion with friends or family is likely.

A coffee shop You can expect a well-earned rest.

A fabric shop A meeting with a helpful person is on the cards.

A greengrocer's shop This dream is an indication of helpful and dependable guests.

A printer's or bookshop You will find success in a creative career.

A wine shop There could be cause for celebration.

Entering a shop This is a good omen denoting prosperity.

Owning a shop Good days are not far away.

Working in a shop You will achieve a reasonable standard in life.

See also **Buying, Selling, Shopkeepers**

Shopping *see* **Buying**

Showers *see* **Rain**

Sickness *see* **Illness**

Silk Silk in a dream is a symbol of a successful partnership and achieving your ambitions.

Buying silk You might expect a sudden financial gain.

Giving or receiving silk This indicates that you will marry a rich partner or your partner will become wealthy.

Silver Silver in any form – whether a coin, silverware or an ingot – symbolises promotion at work.

Buying silver Buying a silver coin denotes a forthcoming marriage in the family, while buying silver ingots means perfect harmony with your partner and parents. Buying silverware suggests either your own marriage to someone wealthy or the marriage of a brother or sister.

Touching silver This indicates a happy marriage and family.
See also **Ingots, Jewellery**

Singing Singing in dreams indicates that a bitter period is to come, marked with unhappiness at home and work.

You are singing If you are singing softly, it predicts disagreements and misunderstandings with your partner. If you are singing loudly, you may receive bad news, perhaps related to your job. If you are alone, you may receive disappointing news from your parents.

Other people are singing You may experience a temporary failure but you will recover.

Sinking Sinking symbolises loss and failure.

A sinking vessel If it is cargo ship, it suggests financial difficulties. A sinking passenger ship indicates a break in partnerships or with friends. A naval vessel sinking suggests that you are feeling hopeless. A small boat sinking is an indication of a temporary problem due to bad advice or bad company.

Being on board a sinking vessel Such a dream warns of impending problems if you do not re-evaluate your plans. It also acts as a warning of undesirable friends. If the boat rights itself and you are saved, it suggests that if you are more realistic you will be able to sort things out.

See also **Boats, Drowning, Quicksand, Ships, Shipwrecks**

Skeletons A skeleton is generally considered an indication of poverty in later life, although it has no significance if you appear very frightened or if you jump in your sleep. If the skeleton gestures towards you, there are hidden dangers around. If the bones are strewn around, it can mean serious illness.

Being a skeleton This is an exceptionally rare dream which suggests that severe problems will cause you anguish.

See also **Bones, Skulls**

Skies

A clear, blue sky Your life will gradually improve and you will have the respect of your colleagues and friends.

A cloudy or grey sky Your efforts are likely to be frustrated by nervousness or stress and you may experience perhaps petty arguments in the family.

Floating in the sky A rare and wonderful dream, this signifies complete relaxation and the end of arguments or disputes.

See also **Moons, Stars**

Skulls A fallen skull can be an indication of ill-health to come, or a warning that if you are already ill you should seek medical advice.

Finding a skull while digging You are likely to receive pleasant news.

Someone holding a skull There is likely to be death around you, although it will not necessarily affect you.

Touching a skull There are arguments in the offing.

See also **Bones, Skeletons**

Smoke

Being in the middle of a cloud of smoke This dream indicates that you will have an unpleasant argument with a friend, which will break up the friendship.

Grey smoke Be more understanding or you will argue with your parents.

Rising black smoke You must be careful to avoid an argument with your partner.

Fast-rising and spreading black smoke This dream foretells serious marital problems unless you take steps to make changes in your relationship.

See also **Burning, Fire**

Smoking *see* **Cigarettes**

Snails If the snail is inside its shell, it is a suggestion of a fickle nature.

A crawling snail This dream indicates irrelevance and laziness in your character. Are you spending too much time on issues which are of no real importance to your life? Several snails crawling together speak of good news.

A dead snail Disappointing news is on its way.

Eating snails Better days are on the way.

Snakes Depending on the circumstances, different interpretations of a snake in a dream are possible.

A single snake Treachery in love is indicated by this dream, emphasised by how close the snake is to you.

A coiled snake The time is right for formulating new and exciting plans.

Large snakes If large snakes, such as boas or anacondas, appear to be threatening you, this suggests you will encounter strong opposition. However, if they are playful or friendly, this is a sign of influential friends.

Several snakes crawling together This symbolises a concerted attempt by colleagues or acquaintances to harm you or your reputation. If you manage to frighten off or even kill the reptile, you will manage to neutralise the negative developments.

A snake harmlessly resting on your shoulders or arms This is a sign of an increase of energy, even if you are elderly.

Holding a snake This indicates immediate recovery from minor ailments or a generally improved level of health.

Being kissed by a snake You could experience a sudden and unexpected financial gain from a source you least expect.

Snow Snow on the ground generally means there is a possibility of an extremely pleasant surprise, perhaps involving money.

Dirty slush An unhappy period should soon come to an end.

Falling snow You will soon find the right person in your life.

Hardened snow You will experience a delay in realising your ambitions.

Running on snow You will receive help from your parents.

Someone falling on snow Use your imagination within limits but be more realistic in your everyday life. If the person is you, be more realistic in your selection of friends.

Walking on snow A wonderful job opportunity will present itself to you.

Soap The appearance of soap in a dream signifies that you are about to start a new activity.

Buying soap You intend to make changes in life or look for a new business partner or colleague.

Touching soap Your latest project could crystallise into a beneficial future.

Using soap on your hands or face You are washing away unpleasant things in the past. You may also look forward to improved health prospects.

Soldiers One or more soldiers in your dream should act as a moral encouragement.
Being a soldier You are in good health and an honest person.
A dead soldier You will suffer a degree of uncertainty.
Soldiers on guard duty You will have a peaceful life.
Soldiers on parade You may soon have reason to celebrate.
Soldiers at war You are likely to receive a surprise, not necessarily an unpleasant one.
Arguing with a soldier Family disputes, perhaps with your father or brother, are likely.
See also **Armies, Fighting, Wars**

Sons If you dream of your eldest son, it means you will enjoy a calm retirement. If you do not have a son but see one in a dream, it is an assurance of help and support and can indicate unexpected gains or prosperity.
Your son giving you something This dream suggests your ambitions will be realised through unexpected help.
Quarrelling with your son Whether or not you actually have a son, this dream indicates that you are acting in too rash a manner with your friends.

Sparrows A flock of sparrows in flight emphasises your fickle nature, while a single one symbolises uncertainty for the foreseeable future.
A chirping sparrow Difficulties may be ahead.
A dead sparrow A difficult period is likely to come to an end.
Feeding sparrows You will have happiness and modest financial security.

Spears You are over-stressed and dissatisfied with your family or friends, and may be feeling a deep animosity towards someone you have disliked for a period of time.
A long spear You are particularly agitated and nervous and should postpone any trips or serious decisions for a couple of weeks.

Holding a spear This dream indicates an impending quarrel. If you threaten someone or injure them, any arguments could be serious and even involve the law.

Receiving a spear You may have contemplated getting what you want in a way you know to be wrong. Do not go against your conscience.

Spiders A spider symbolises protection from harm and also the encouragement to live a good life. Two or more spiders is a sign that you should continue in a righteous way of life.

A dead spider This is an encouragement to think more carefully about the morals of your recent behaviour.

Killing a spider This is a harsh reminder that your attitude to life is not realistic and should be reviewed.

A spider spinning a web You will find a way out of a difficult situation, or a decision you have been expecting will be made in your favour. If the spider is hanging from the web, you will find a bad period for you will come to an end, and if the spider is within the web, you will be protected from harm, whatever its source.

See also **Cobwebs**

Spiders' webs *see* **Cobwebs**

Spots *see* **Acne**

Stables A stable with a single animal indicates some kind of breakthrough connected with work. If there are several animals, it shows that you will do reasonably well financially and will be contented and have plenty of friends, although if the animals are all donkeys, you will have to work very hard to gain anything.

Building or repairing a stable You will follow a traditional path in life.

See also **Donkeys, Horses**

Stairs A narrow, winding staircase symbolises a favourable surprise, while a straight, narrow staircase indicates the opposite.

A door at the end of stairs The future is bright, but if you reach the end of the stairs and open the door on to an empty room, your efforts are not properly directed. If the room is full of friendly people, however, it is a sign of prosperity and happiness.

Falling downstairs You are likely to experience a loss of some kind.
Being pushed downstairs Be warned to choose your friends with care, although any attempts to cause you harm are unlikely to be successful.

Stars Bright, shining stars spell happy moments, with advancement at work. If the stars are dull, you will have to work very hard to achieve anything. If the stars appear to be very close to you, it denotes continued good health and a happy marriage, whether or not you are already married.
Falling stars A sudden failure and failing health are indicated by this dream. It could also indicate misunderstandings with your partner or children, if you have them.

Starvation A dream of contrary meaning, this symbolises plenty, prosperity and property.
You are starving This dream heralds an excellent beginning with plenty of money and property. If you appear to be nearing death, you are likely to be able to realise your ambitions and have enough to be able to offer substantial help to those less fortunate than you. If someone appears to pity you, it underlines your selfless nature.
Seeing others starving Whoever the starving people are, they will be happy and want for nothing. If you help them in your dream, it underlines your compassionate nature.
See also **Famine, Hunger**

Stately homes *see* **Mansions, Palaces**

Statues Seeing in a dream a statue that you have contemplated in life indicates a consistent nature. If you cannot identify it, the posture and material of the statue are important.
A beautiful statue with friendly features You will receive support from friends.
A bronze statue You could experience misunderstandings with your partner.
A clay or plaster statue You may experience some health problems, although they will not necessarily be serious.
A damaged or angry-looking statue This is a warning of potential problems in some sphere of your life.
A golden statue You tend to be reckless in your behaviour.

A marble statue You will enjoy success at work.

A stone statue You will have good health.

Stitching *see* Sewing

Stockings For a woman to see new stockings, it suggests successful love affairs. For a man to dream of stockings tends to suggest irresponsibility.

Buying stockings This dream indicates an awareness of the importance of planning for the future.

Putting on stockings You will have a unique husband.

Torn or laddered stockings You are likely to be disappointed in love at some time in the near future.

Stonemasons *see* Bricklayers

Straw

Cut straw on a field You should be careful of negligence or you will suffer loss.

A field of straw This symbolises a good salary or a better standard of living if you are flexible and sensible.

Straw in bales heaped together You may be disappointed in love or have arguments with your partner.

Straw bales lying apart in a field A separation is likely.

Burning straw This dream indicates problems in the near future, probably as a result of your own actions. If you manage to put out the fire alone, you have a last-minute chance to turn over a new leaf. If others help you fight the blaze, you will receive wise advice and even help to start again. If the fire appears to be put out without damaging the straw, then a timely and wise move will resolve any impending problems.

See also Farms

Strawberries This beautiful fruit symbolises true friendship, good health and happiness.

A field of strawberries You will have a generally happy and uneventful life.

A plate or basket full of strawberries You have trustworthy and dependable friends.

Rotten strawberries You are not utilising all the opportunities available to you.

Buying or serving strawberries You will have a good life.
Eating strawberries Your good health will continue or even
improve.

Suffocation Being in danger of suffocation denotes family feuds
that require sorting out.
See also **Danger**

Suicide Suicide by any means is an indication that you should seek
help and advice to pull you out of your depressive state.
Committing suicide You have lost hope after a series of failures.
Others committing suicide You are over-stressed and may
regret a hasty decision.
Thinking about committing suicide You are harbouring a deep
resentment against someone.

Sunflowers A single sunflower indicates financial gain while a field
of sunflowers means your efforts will be partially successful.
Dead or drooping sunflowers The means by which you are
trying to advance your finances should be reviewed.

Swans
A black swan You should enjoy good health, a sound marriage
and a happy family.
A white swan You will have a respectable position in life and
family happiness.
Feeding a swan An early success is likely to be yours.
A dead swan Your attitude to life is hopeless or despairing; try
to take steps to change the way you are feeling.

Swearing
Other people swearing You should avoid stressful situations at
home otherwise there are likely to be arguments.
You are swearing You need to keep tighter control over your
actions otherwise you may find that your fortunes take a
downward turn.

Swimming If you are swimming in a small pond or a pool, you
should be moderately successful. Swimming in a calm river
denotes good health, but in a turbulent river, it indicates minor
disputes which could bring health problems or make you feel

low. Swimming in the sea indicates a likely trip to the coast which will be beneficial.

Getting into difficulty while swimming You are likely to experience difficulties before things get better. If someone helps you, you will receive help or support.

See also **Drowning, Lakes, Life-saving, Oceans, Rivers, Water**

Swords If sheathed, a sword in a dream is a timely warning to control your temper. If unsheathed, it suggests serious arguments and perhaps even violence.

Attacking someone with a sword This suggests that you will be involved in arguments or even legal proceedings, which will not be successful for you. Take steps to reduce your stress levels and control your anger and things will improve.

You are given a sword Some people you consider to be friends are in fact untrustworthy and you should not be guided by them.

Being attacked with a sword Be on your guard against people who do not have your best interests at heart.

Buying a sword You may be considering something misguided or even illegal.

Selling a sword You have decided not to do something you would have regretted.

See also **Cuts, Wounds**

Synagogues *see* **Religious buildings**

T

Tables A large table with several unoccupied chairs suggests an imminent meeting with family or friends that will be beneficial. If you have been involved in an argument with your partner, this dream could also signal the end to the misunderstandings.

A table set for two A good marriage is indicated.

A table with broken crockery or bottles There may be misunderstandings between friends, or family quarrels.

An empty table without chairs Much will have to be done to achieve a little.

A table spread with cakes for tea This dream suggests good friendships.

A table spread for dinner You will have a happy domestic life.

A table with flowers If the flowers are strewn across the table, there will be a period of mourning or sadness, although if they are arranged in a vase, it is an indication of success.

A table with empty plates You are in a state of confusion, especially if the table is covered with things that should not be there.

See also **Desks**

Tailors Seeing a tailor working encourages you to use your talents constructively. If he or she is sitting around doing nothing, you have been intensely discouraged by past failures.

Being a tailor You are finally on your way towards a better future. If someone is helping you, you will be able to rely on your friends.

A tailor measuring you for new clothes You will soon hear good news, but if the tailor tells you that it is not possible to make your clothes, you may have financial or social problems unless you move quickly to rectify the situation.

A tailor tells you that your clothes are ready This is a favourable sign of a promotion or some other success.

Arguing with a tailor Your behaviour is often irresponsible.

See also **Sewing**

Talking If you are talking loudly or aggressively in your dream, you may be under intense pressure and finding it difficult to cope. You are likely to remain lonely unless you find ways to cope with stress.

Talking loudly but happily Money could be coming your way.

Talking very softly You are not sure of your next step in life.

Talking to your family Members of your family are likely to be able to help you.

Talking to a business associate This is a good sign in your work environment.

Talking with friends A short but pleasant trip is likely.

Talking to your partner This dream indicates the imminent arrival of guests.

Tanks, armoured *see* **Weapons**

Taxis

Climbing into a taxi Something you have been waiting for is about to begin. If the driver does not speak, things are likely to turn out fairly well for you, but if he or she says the journey will be difficult, you may encounter problems along the way.

Driving aimlessly around in a taxi You have a strong desire to achieve success but have yet to focus on how you will do so.

Getting out of a taxi A successful project is coming to an end.

Hailing a taxi You have a hasty nature and a desire to get things done quickly.

Tea Dreaming of tea generally indicates unhappiness and a period marked by arguments.

Drinking tea If you are alone, any problems you encounter are likely to be of your own making. If you are with friends or colleagues, it is more likely that someone else is responsible for your failures. If you are with your parents, you can expect a tense period in the family. If you are with your partner, it can indicate arguments.

Making tea This reflects a nervous and unhappy nature.

Being invited for tea This dream is a good sign indicating pleasant surprises.

Teachers A teacher is a symbol of both caution and patience. If you see your current teacher, you should be careful in your day-to-day affairs and not do anything stupid. If you see an old teacher from the past, it is a sign that your patience will be rewarded.

Being a teacher Your hard work will yield positive results as it is better to be sensible than unrealistic.
See also **Schools**

Tears *see* **Crying, Eyes**

Teeth Dirty or discoloured teeth signify ill-health, although not serious, while perfect teeth indicate continued good health, or recovery if you have not been well.
Teeth all around you Be more careful in your dealings.
Teeth falling out If you dream your teeth are falling out one by one, you are likely to exchange a greedy life for a more spiritual one, but if you dream of a single tooth being extracted or falling out, you may lose an important friend through your own stupidity. If you are injured and dream of teeth falling out, it has no prophetic significance.

Telephones
Telephoning a friend Make sure you have planned things well, otherwise you will have problems.
Telephoning your parents If you are telephoning your parents to ask for help, it underlines the fact that you are in an unhappy period of your life. If they console you, then help will come through the intervention of others. If they tell you off because of the circumstances in which you find yourself, then you will have to make the first move or you will not receive the help you need. If they praise you, be cautious in your approach to life. If the conversation is just an exchange of greetings, things are not as bad as you think.
Telephoning your partner or children Family life is very important to you.
Receiving a call If someone tells you there is a call for you but you cannot find the telephone, someone is trying to harm you. If you answer a call from your partner or children, it underlines the deep importance you feel for family life.
Receiving a threatening call If you recognise the person calling you, beware of jealousy surrounding you.

Temples *see* **Religious buildings**

Tents Several tents indicate hectic activity.

Tents being taken down A time of idleness is coming to an end.

Tents on fire A change of location will be beneficial to you.

Being inside a tent Being alone in a tent indicates a temporary relief from difficulties, perhaps with help from an unexpected source. If you are with people you do not recognise, you are likely to meet someone who will benefit you in some way. If it is raining outside while you are safe inside, some relief will come because of your foresight.

Erecting a tent If you are alone, you will have to work hard for what you have. If you have help, you will have good friends.

A tent collapses on you Something you have done has caused your misfortunes. Change your direction and you will be able to avert difficulties.

Thorns Thorns symbolise obstacles and problems created by your own obstinacy or irresponsibility. Try to avoid setting unrealistic goals. If you are near a thorn bush, you will encounter many obstacles unless you become more realistic and reliable.

Being hurt by thorns If you are hurt, a calm period is ahead, but if you bleed, it is a sign of loss due to negligence and a warning to choose reliable friends.

Thunder If you hear thunder nearby, it is a good sign symbolising the beginning of a new phase in your life. If the noise is faint and the thunder is at a distance, it can be an indication of a sadness approaching. If you have argued with someone close to you, take steps to resolve your differences.

Someone tells you they have heard thunder There will soon be an end to misunderstandings with former friends.

Tigers A tiger in a cage indicates your careful behaviour.

A tiger approaches you aggressively Take this as a warning to keep away from anyone suspicious.

A tiger attacks you You can expect serious misunderstandings with your friends, but if you manage to frighten it away, you will be able to avoid unsavoury acquaintances.

Tights *see* **Stockings**

Toads Seeing a toad near you in a dream indicates a strong temptation to get what you want by dishonest means. The further away the animal is from you, the less the temptation.
Killing a toad Either killing a toad or seeing a dead one emphasises that you have the ability to resist the temptation to act immorally or dishonestly.

Tomatoes A field of tomatoes symbolises continued good health.
Eating tomatoes You will recover from ill-health.
Buying tomatoes Good news is on the way, perhaps a positive response to a request.
Being offered tomatoes Good friends will support you when you most need them.
Offering or selling tomatoes You have the determination to start a new phase in your life. Use the energy wisely and it will be successful.

Torches A shining torch in your hand, or switching on a torch, indicates the respect you earn by your sociable attitude.
A torchlight suddenly goes out This is a warning that you should not be tempted to do anything you know is wrong.
Someone tries to stop you switching on a torch or tries to switch off your torch Someone may try to thwart your plans but they are unlikely to be successful.

Tortoises Tortoises in dreams symbolise honesty and good health and your determination to maintain a strong moral sense.
Feeding or playing with a tortoise You will have a long and healthy life.
Lifting or carrying a tortoise Your life will be modest but good.
A dead tortoise Resist the temptation to act against the dictates of your own good conscience.

Towers Courage, determination and honesty are symbolised by a tower in your dreams. If you pass one, stand near it or see it from a short distance, it should reassure you that your self-confidence is justified.
A partly ruined tower Take this as an encouragement to hope for the best. If the tower is completely ruined, you are likely to experience a temporary setback but you will overcome it with presence of mind.

Entering a tower You will work hard to achieve your ambitions. If the tower is made of red brick, there may be some delay in fulfilling your ambitions.

Trains Determination, prosperity and happiness are generally indicated by seeing a train in a dream.

A moving train If the train speeds past you, better times are on their way. If it is a goods train, this will relate to the world of work. A passenger train presages a beneficial meeting, although if the train appears to be empty, you must be careful not to be too trusting.

A derailed train This dream warns you to be more realistic and careful or you are likely to suffer loss of some kind.

A stationary train You are determined to make things better for yourself. A goods train suggests success at work, while a passenger train heralds the arrival of friends. If you are walking towards a stationary train or waiting to board one at a station, a short journey will have a big influence on your life.

Boarding a train If it is easy, your approach to life is realistic but if you have difficulty boarding the train, a change of attitude would be helpful to you.

Being on a train You may not feel that you are in an advantageous situation but you will soon realise that things are going well. If another train is running parallel to the train you are on, it is a sign of support from friends or family. If the tracks suddenly diverge, you will experience a short period of anxiety but it will not have any serious implications. If you see a train passing in the opposite direction, it is a promising sign of a resolution to an argument with a partner or member of your family.

Riding on a train through a city or a village You will unexpectedly come across an old friend.

Riding on a train passing through a desert You will soon discover new opportunities.

Riding on a train through a jungle or forest You need to settle any outstanding matters, otherwise they will become the source of continued annoyance.

Eating on a train Whether alone or with other people, this denotes that you are fairly contented with the way your life is going.

See also **Travelling**

Tramps Dreaming of a tramp means you should be careful of unscrupulous people around you.

Being a tramp You are guilty of irresponsible behaviour, perhaps towards your partner.

Talking with a tramp If the tramp gestures to you or speaks to you, there may be a sad circumstance ahead, possibly concerning your family. If you speak to the tramp, it is an indication of your own uncertainty.

Arguing with a tramp Your life will take a turn for the better.

Giving something to a tramp If you do not speak to the tramp, this indicates a sudden change in your life, probably for the better.

Receiving something from a tramp You are about to encounter a difficulty ahead.

Traps Whatever form the trap takes, it is a sign that you should be aware of what is going on around you if you want to avoid unpleasant developments.

Being trapped You may have to face legal problems.

Laying a trap Laying a trap for others reflects a vicious streak in your character.

A dead animal in a trap Your so-called friends may be the cause of some of your problems and you should choose your associates with care.

A live animal in a trap You will be able to extricate yourself from difficulties.

Travellers *see* **Gypsies**

Travelling

Travelling on business or pleasure Things will ultimately work out well if you remain patient.

Travelling with a colleague Things will go well at work and you may even get a promotion.

Travelling with your family or partner You are likely to have a happy home life.

Travelling to escape from something Stress may cause arguments.

Travelling to get away from your children You have been too passive in tackling your problems.

Treasure Treasures featuring in a dream can have either favourable or unfavourable interpretations, depending on the circumstances.

Finding treasure by chance You are likely to receive money through an inheritance or chance.

Hunting for treasure If you dream that you look for treasure and find it, it can indicate a favourable business deal in the near future.

Others finding treasure If someone tells you they have found treasure, you are likely to meet an influential friend.

Others digging for treasure This is a sign of encouragement, although if they are quarrelling, this can mean arguments in real life, either at work or at home, if you do not proceed with caution.

Trees Trees generally symbolise growth, prosperity, emotions and ability. A well-foliaged fruit tree with unripe fruit indicates improvement at work and dependable friends and family. If the fruit is ripe, or if you see a tree in flower, it suggests that you will achieve your goals in the end, even though you may have to wait.

A bare tree Your life will be unfulfilled unless you make changes.

Fir trees You will enjoy continued good health.

Palm trees You will take a trip that will be of benefit to you.

Oak trees These are indications of strength, good health and a happy and contented life.

A walnut tree This tree signifies quarrels.

A yew trees This is an indication of good luck.

A dead tree This underlines your worries for the past and reminds you to look to the future.

Withered or damaged trees Whatever the type of tree, this dream indicates that you are likely to experience a period of difficulty.

Climbing a tree If you are climbing easily, you will have success, although if you are finding it hard, you may have difficulty facing up to life's realities. If someone asks you to climb a tree and you accept, it means you will soon receive an employment opportunity that may change your life drastically. If you refuse to climb, it means you are missing out on opportunities because of your attitude.

Falling from a tree Your behaviour tends to be careless.

See also **Digging, Forests, Leaves**

Tunnels Hope, a temporary setback or uncertainty can all be indicated by dreaming of a tunnel, depending on the circumstances.

The mouth of a tunnel A general setback is indicated by a dream of the mouth of a dark tunnel, although it is likely to be only temporary. If the tunnel is lit, then you are likely to overcome your difficulties through determination.

Inside a tunnel If the tunnel is dark, your acquaintances are likely to be the cause of any problems you experience. If you are frightened or lost, you are likely to undergo a period of uncertainly, perhaps caused by your own bad planning. If you see a light or an exit, however, even at a distance, someone you least expect may help you out of your difficulties.

See also **Darkness**

Turkeys A turkey symbolises unreliable friends.

A cackling turkey This dream warns of indecent acquaintances and suggests that you should not pin your hopes on other people's promises.

A feeding turkey People will try to spoil your plans but will be unsuccessful.

Eating turkey meat You will overcome your adversity peacefully.

Tying *see* **Knots, Ropes**

u

Umbrellas Seeing an umbrella in a dream can symbolise hope or hopelessness, financial gains or loss, or protection from harm.

A closed umbrella A closed umbrella on the floor indicates that you are feeling hopeless about an aspect of your life, but if it is upright or leaning against a wall, then you are feeling more positive.

An open umbrella A careful disposition is indicated by using an umbrella in the rain, and may also bring the hope of financial gain. However, if it is not raining, it is an indication of some kind of false dealing. If someone holds an umbrella over you, regardless of the weather, it indicates that you will receive moral, or perhaps financial, support in the near future.

Attacking someone with an umbrella Attacking someone, or being attacked, with an umbrella means that you will have to face any problems in life alone.

Breaking an umbrella This is a sign of hopelessness and the need for a change of direction.

Buying an umbrella You have a careful attitude to life and to money. If you see yourself in a shop with several umbrellas, you can expect support from your family.

Forgetting an umbrella Forgetting your umbrella means that you may receive a small gift from someone in your family.

Losing an umbrella and searching for it You may suffer a financial loss, although not necessarily a significant one.

Uncles Dreaming of your uncle is a good sign of solutions to problems, especially if he gives you a gift. If you give him something or are engaged in friendly conversation, you'll find a way through your difficulties, however much the odds seem stacked against you at the moment.

Undressing Any interpretation of this dream is determined by the reason for the action. Undressing at home or in private suggests you will not succeed in what you are working on at the moment; undressing in public indicates problems ahead.

Undressing someone else Undressing someone of the opposite sex means you do not fully understand the realities of your current situation.

Being undressed If you are being undressed against your will, it is an indication that you should be especially careful in your decision-making, as the wrong decision could have unfortunate consequences.
Seeing others undressing This dream is a likely indication of ill-health or difficulties at work.
See also **Clothes, Nakedness**

Unfaithfulness *see* **Infidelity**

Unhappiness This is a dream of contrary meaning, which actually indicates joy and success. If the reason you are unhappy in your dream relates to a circumstance you have experienced in real life, your patience will be rewarded and things will turn out all right.

Uniforms If you wear a uniform in life and see yourself in that uniform in your dream, it means that things will continue to go along fairly well for you. However, if the uniform is torn or dirty, you need to think about changing your circumstances in order to improve things. If you do not normally wear a uniform and dream of wearing one, especially if it is a military uniform, it is an indication that you are unhappy with your present situation or worrying about something in your past.

Urinating This is a sign of nervousness and unhappiness. If you are in a toilet, you will solve your problems, but if you are outside or in a public place, then it indicates a severe degree of uneasiness.
Others urinating Again, this dream indicates some fear or nervousness within you. If anyone urinates on you, it shows their ingratitude towards you, and if they threaten to do so, it shows that you should be careful of friends whose motives towards you are not always good.

V

Valleys

A cultivated valley Any success is likely to be gained with relative ease.

A deep and barren valley You may be offered the possibility of entering into the world of business.

A deep, forested valley You will earn success through hard work.

A shallow, barren valley This is often a sign of a sense of isolation.

A shallow, forested valley Your domestic situation may be causing you to feel uneasy.

Being in a valley If you are alone in a green valley, you will bring any project to fruition on your own. If you are with anyone else, then you are likely to receive the help of friends and colleagues. Standing, alone or with others, in a barren valley is a suggestion that you should replan your next step as it may not be successful for you.

See also **Countryside**

Vases

A large vase The time is favourable for a new beginning in your life.

A vase containing flowers You are likely to gain help and encouragement from friends.

A broken vase You are likely to encounter a problem with your plans.

Being given a vase Your work is progressing well and will lead to success in the end.

Giving a vase You will realise your ambitions to such an extent that you will then be able to help other people.

Veils A veil is a symbol of hypocrisy and lies.

Someone wearing a veil Any suspicions you have of other people's dishonesty are likely to be well founded. If the veil is torn, you can look to find proof of your suspicions quite quickly.

Being veiled You are hiding something or acting dishonestly.

Verses *see* **Poetry**

VILLAGES

Villages Seeing a village from a distance suggests an inner
tranquillity. If it is close by, it is an indication of a wonderful
married life.
An abandoned village You are likely to suffer a serious
disappointment.
Being in a village This dream reflects your contentment and
underlines your honest and friendly nature. This is emphasised if
you speak with people in the village.

Vineyards A beautifully laid-out vineyard full of grapes signifies
sudden financial gain, possibly through an inheritance. A
vineyard without grapes on the vines indicates a time of
uncertainty due to poor planning. If the vines are withered, it
suggests loss, which will be more severe if the vines are damaged
or burnt.
Walking in a vineyard You can think and act constructively if
you make the effort.
See also **Grapes**

Violets Violets in a field suggest good news, a job opportunity or
better health.
Holding violets in your hands A happy marriage or a marriage
proposal is indicated.
Being offered violets Your life will improve in some significant
way.

Violins A period of harmony in the family is likely, especially if you
touch the violin.
Playing a violin You will soon recover from any health
problems you have experienced.
Someone playing a violin Especially if they are a family
member, this dream indicates a new relationship for someone
close to you. It also signifies perfect harmony at home. However,
if you do not recognise the person playing the violin, it can
indicate quarrels.

Visits
Visiting others Visiting friends in a friendly atmosphere
suggests the beginning of a new and fruitful project. Visiting
your parents symbolises your serious approach to life. Visiting
uncles or other family members suggests success for yourself

and your family. Visiting a doctor as a friend rather than as a patient suggests good health. Visiting your employer as a guest indicates success and the resolution of problems at work. Visiting your siblings denotes continued encouragement, while visiting in-laws suggests continuing good relations with your family.
Receiving visitors A visit by your parents reflects the respect you command, while a visit from friends suggests modest but successful ventures connected with work or business. A visit by a doctor suggest a health problem. Visits by aunts or in-laws indicate a possible misunderstanding that could be resolved through patience and good sense.

Vultures A vulture is an ominous symbol, indicating revenge and animosity. If the vulture is flying, you should be careful of vengeful people. If it is on the ground, your detractors are on the verge of harming you unless you take great care.
An aggressive vulture Arguments are likely in the near future.
Vultures feeding You would be well advised to change your life or expect negative consequences.
A dead vulture Your enemies will not succeed in any plans against you.

W

Walking Walking at leisure suggests the successful end to a project, but walking quickly as if you are evading someone means a period of uncertainty.
Walking on a flat and deserted path You need to consider changing your approach if you do not wish to risk isolation.
Walking on a grassy path or in the countryside You can expect good health, financial success and good friends.
Walking towards any means of transport This dream symbolises an urge to change your life.
Walking with others If you recognise your companions, you will do well because of the support you receive from others. If you do not recognise them, you will have to rely on your own ability. Walking with your partner and children means important and constructive decisions will be taken soon.

Walls A wall blocking your path or enclosing you indicates obstacles and problems at work.
Leaning idly against a wall Any misunderstandings or difficulties are not likely to be quickly resolved.
Trying to a climb a wall You are eager to overcome your problems.

Wandering If you are despondent and unhappy, you are likely to tackle your problems wisely and over the next couple of months you will achieve results that are likely to satisfy you, even though they may not be the perfect resolution. If in real life you are contented, then this dream can indicate a level of greed.

Warehouses Seeing a warehouse in your dream indicates an improvement in your financial status. If you are in a warehouse and satisfied with the way your stock is being stored, it indicates profit.

Wars Contrary to what it implies, war in a dream symbolises peace, happiness and friendship.
Hearing about war Hearing that war has been declared is a sign of calm and peace and happiness in the family. If two or more

countries in your dream are already at war, it indicates success and prosperity.

Experiencing war You are ready for a rebirth in your life. The presence of blood eliminates any prophetic significance.

See also **Fighting, Soldiers, Weapons**

Washing *see* **Bathing, Soap**

Wasps A wasp is not an auspicious element in a dream as it indicates that someone may be working behind your back and you may receive bad news. If there is more than one wasp in your dream, be cautious in your dealings with anyone you suspect may not have your best interests at heart.

A wasp menacing you or stinging you You may be worried by malicious rumours spread by people you once trusted.

Killing a wasp You will find your way out of your problems.

Watches *see* **Clocks**

Water Good health, success and a happy marriage are indicated by dreams of clean water. A clear expanse of water symbolises good health and a modest or good future.

Dirty or muddy water Your situation is undecided and you may be confused by conflicting feelings.

Clear, flowing water There are possibilities for exploiting positive forces within you.

Being in water If the water is clear or drinkable, you are likely to have successful relationships and a good marriage. If it is dirty or muddy, quarrels or misunderstandings between you and your friends or family are likely.

Drinking water If the water is clear, it suggests an early recovery from a minor illness. If it is dirty, it suggests a minor illness.

See also **Drowning, Floods and flooding, Rivers, Swimming**

Wealth If you are poor or only moderately well-off in real life and dream of being suddenly wealthy, it indicates that you will have enough money, although if you are wealthy and have this dream, it can indicate that greed could lead you to lose what you have.

See also **Money**

Weaving *see* **Carpets**

Weapons This dream refers to any heavy weapons with the potential for mass destruction, from ancient cannons to modern artillery, bombs or tanks. Whether it is a good or a bad omen depends on the circumstances in which you see the weapons in your dreams. If you are confronted with major difficulties in your life, this indicates that you have the power to overcome them. However, if you are about to embark on a large-scale investment or major business activity, it should be taken as a reminder to rethink and make sure that you are right to go ahead at this time.
Weapons being fired This is a warning that you should avoid unnecessary risks in your business dealings. It also signals that you may suffer a loss as a result of past transactions.
Weapons being fired at you You have been showing a negative and timid attitude to life. Take steps to improve your self-image and build up your levels of assertiveness and you will find it will be to your advantage.
See also **Arrows, Daggers, Guns, Knives, Spears, Swords**

Wells Seeing a well reminds you not to indulge in dubious activities as they will not benefit you. If there is water in the well, the chances are that you will come to your senses, but if the well is dry, you will have to answer to those around you for any immoral acts you have committed.
Being in a well If the well is dry, you alone are responsible for your difficulties. If the well is full of water and you could drown, a difficult period may well be in store for you.
Being rescued from a well Someone will help you in life.

Wheelbarrows Seeing a wheelbarrow or old-fashioned handcart of any kind is a symbol of achieving success through sheer hard work. Since it is usually pushed or pulled by one person, the dream indicates that you will have to manage without the help of others if you are to succeed. Alternatively, it could indicate that you are dogged in your refusal to accept other people's help.
Pulling or pushing a wheelbarrow Although this is a good sign that you have begun to move in the right direction, there's plenty of work to do before you get where you want to be. If the

route you are following appears to be uphill, you will encounter temporary difficulties, whereas if you are moving downhill, you will find things slightly easier.

*A **wheelbarrow moving on its own*** Your life is likely to get better in the near future, either financially or in your personal circumstances and relationships.

Whips Holding a whip symbolises the intense anger within you.

Whipping someone This dream reflects a long-standing animosity. You need to be more tolerant of others.

Being whipped You need to become more active in working towards what you want. If you attack the person who is whipping you, you will make a last-minute attempt to make changes that will be to your own benefit.

Whistling If you have a dream that you are whistling, you have already gained considerable success but may be unaware of it. If you are very unhappy in real life, then you will soon feel happier and more content.

Other people are whistling Others will benefit from your stupidity unless you act more sensibly.

Widows There is only a significance to seeing a widow in a dream if you recognise her. If you are planning to marry soon, this dream can indicate misunderstandings with your future spouse, which will need to be handled carefully.

Speaking with a widow You may find circumstances arise in the near future that are not to your liking but you should be able to overcome any difficulties with common sense and a careful attitude.

Windows A window in a dream relates to status and future possibilities.

A broken window You are feeling angry and need to practise calm.

An open window If you approach an open window, it means you will gain further respect and status in society. If someone opens it for you, look out for a number of opportunities that you could turn to your advantage. If the window is only half-open, you may have difficulties taking advantage of the opportunity.

A closed window Your social activities are likely to come to a temporary halt, although if you then open the window wide, things will improve.

Looking out of a window If you see someone friendly approaching, you will meet new and helpful people. If someone throws something at you, those around you are not always on your side.

Wine If you are drinking wine with friends, it is a sign of modest success, but if you are drinking alone you may have domestic problems.

Other people drinking wine You are too lethargic and should be more aware of what is going on around you.

Being invited to drink wine You will soon meet with appreciable success.

See also **Bottles, Drinking**

Witches Seeing a witch means you must expect some unpredictable developments, but if the witch approaches you and exchanges a word of greeting, or asks if she can help you, the majority of your problems will be solved to your satisfaction.

A witch gives you something This rare dream means a financial gain or gift of some kind.

Being a witch You have the potential to be more socially useful.

Arguing with a witch Quarrels with friends are likely.

Wives A wife symbolises courage, support and calm. If you are unhappy or sick and she offers you encouragement or support, then you will soon feel better. Whatever is happening in your life is likely to improve.

Wolves If you see a wolf in a dream, it is said to be a sign of bad luck. If the wolf approaches you, whether menacingly or not, it suggests that someone you considered a good friend may turn out to be an enemy.

Frightening or killing a wolf You will find a way to avoid false rumours being spread about you.

Wounds

A wound on your abdomen You are likely to suffer a short illness.

184

A wound on your back Some of your friends or colleagues may be untrustworthy.

A wound on your hand You could encounter a temporary problem either in your social activities or at work.

A wound on your knee You may suffer financial loss.

A wound on your legs or feet You will have temporary problems with work-related travel.

A wound on your navel You will enjoy success in business or at work.

A wound on your stomach You are getting too greedy.

See also **Cuts, Daggers, Knives, Swords**

Wreaths A wreath indicates the end of a difficult period and therefore the start of something new that may change your life.

Writing

Writing letters This dream is a sign of good news, hope and support.

Writing a text or manuscript You have a good deal of patience but also a feeling of sadness.

Seeing others writing You will make a timely intervention in someone's affairs which is likely to be to everyone's benefit.

See also **Poetry**

Z

Zebras If you see a zebra grazing or at rest, it means that you will
have an uncertain future and should choose your career path
carefully. If the animal is running, expect a sudden change in
your life.

*A **herd** of zebras* You are about to enter a difficult period, which
you will have to face with careful planning.

*A **dead** zebra* You will soon come to the end of a bad period;
financial and social improvements are just over the horizon.

Zits *see* **Acne**

Index